I0235232

40
War Office
2052

[Crown Copyright Reserved.

INFANTRY TRAINING.

(4-COMPANY ORGANIZATION.)

1914.

GENERAL STAFF, WAR OFFICE.

LONDON:
PRINTED UNDER THE AUTHORITY OF HIS MAJESTY'S STATIONERY OFFICE
By HARRISON AND SONS, 45-47, ST. MARTIN'S LANE, W.C.,
PRINTERS IN ORDINARY TO HIS MAJESTY.

To be purchased, either directly or through any Bookseller, from
WYMAN AND SONS, LTD., 29, BREAMS BUILDINGS, FETTER LANE, E.C., and
54, ST. MARY STREET CARDIFF ; or
H.M. STATIONERY OFFICE (SCOTTISH BRANCH), 23, FORTH STREET, EDINBURGH ; or
E. PONSONBY, LTD., 116, GRAFTON STREET, DUBLIN ;
or from the Agencies in the British Colonies and Dependencies,
the United States of America, the Continent of Europe and Abroad of
T. FISHER UNWIN, LONDON, W.C.

1914.

Price Sixpence.

This Manual is issued by command of the Army Council, and deals with the training of Infantry and its leading in war.

The attention of commanders is drawn to "Training and Manœuvre Regulations," Section 2.

Any enunciation by officers responsible for training of principles other than those contained in this Manual, or any practice of methods not based on those principles, is forbidden.

[signature]

WAR OFFICE,

10th August, 1914.

(n 10984) Wt. 23313-179   200 M   10/14.   H & S   P. 13/461

CONTENTS.

(B 10984)   A 2

1. SQUAD DRILL WITHOUT ARMS.

SQUAD DRILL WITH INTERVALS.

SQUAD DRILL IN SINGLE RANK.

SQUAD DRILL IN TWO RANKS.

2. SQUAD DRILL WITH ARMS.

RIFLE EXERCISES.

CHAPTER III.
SECTION AND PLATOON DRILL.

PLATOON DRILL.

CHAPTER IV.
COMPANY DRILL.

CHAPTER V.
EXTENDED ORDER DRILL.

CHAPTER VI.
· BATTALION DRILL.

CHAPTER XV.

MACHINE GUNS IN BATTLE.

CHAPTER XVI.

AMMUNITION SUPPLY.　ENTRENCHING TOOLS.

APPENDIX I.
INSTRUCTION IN BAYONET FIGHTING.

APPENDIX II.
SYLLABUS FOR A 6 MONTHS' COURSE OF RECRUIT TRAINING.

LIST OF PLATES.

ORGANIZATION AND DEFINITIONS.

i. *Organization.*

1. An infantry brigade consists of :—
   Headquarters.
   4 Infantry battalions.

2. A battalion consists of :—
   Headquarters.
   Machine gun section.
   4 companies.

For purposes of administration the details of battalion head-quarters (other than the battalion commander, senior major, adjutant, and quartermaster) and the machine gun section are posted to companies as supernumerary to the establishment of platoons. Their distribution among the companies is at the discretion of the battalion commander but should be so arranged that the number of supernumeraries in each company is approximately equal.

3. A company consists of 4 platoons*, and is commanded by a major or mounted captain, with a captain as second in command.

4. A platoon consists of 4 sections, and is commanded by a subaltern, with a serjeant as second in command (platoon serjeant). Platoons are numbered consecutively throughout the battalion from 1 to 16.

---

* In certain battalions with a special establishment the number of platoons in a company varies from two to four

When a subaltern is not available to command, the platoon serjeant will take his place, but in this case a section commander will not be taken from his command to act as platoon serjeant. The transfer of a platoon serjeant to another platoon should be as infrequent as possible.

So far as the exigencies of peace conditions will admit, this organization will be maintained both in barracks and in the field for all duties, including the detailing of fatigues. The men will thus acquire the spirit of comradeship, and learn to repose confidence in each other, while the section commanders will be accustomed to command, and to act when necessary on their own judgment.

5. A section is commanded by a non-commissioned officer, and is the normal fire-unit. Sections are numbered consecutively throughout the company from 1 to 16, and the men of each section should be kept together in barracks as well as in the field. The post of section commander is a definite appointment, and transfers should be as infrequent as possible.

ii. *Definitions.*

Alignment.—Any straight line on which a body of troops is formed, or is to form.

Column.—Bodies of troops on parallel and successive alignments, at a distance from one another equal to their own frontage, *e.g.* column of companies or column of platoons.

Column of masses.—See under masses.

Column of route.—A column of fours with not more than four men abreast in any part of the column, including officers and supernumeraries. The normal formation for troops marching on a road.

Close column.—A column with distances reduced to suit requirements. If no specific orders are given, the distance between units will be seven paces.

Double column.—Two parallel columns, with any named interval between them.

Deploy, to.—To change formation from column or close column into line on the same alignment.

Depth.—The space occupied by a body of troops from front to rear.

Direction (battalion, company, platoon, section, or file of).—The battalion, company, platoon, section, or file responsible for keeping the direction in a drill movement.

Distance.—The space between units in column or close column, measured from the heels of the front rank of one unit to the heels of the front rank of the next.

Dress, to.—To take up the alignment correctly.

Drill.—The training of the soldier to execute certain movements as a second nature.

Echelon.—A formation of successive and parallel units facing in the same direction, each on a flank and to the rear of the unit in front of it.

File.—A front rank man and his rear rank man.

Fire unit.—Any number of men firing by the executive command of one. The section is the normal fire unit.

Flank, directing.—The flank by which units march or dress.

Flank, inner.—That nearer to the directing flank.

Flank, outer.—That opposite to the inner or directing flank.

Formation (Battalion, company, platoon, section, or file of).—The battalion, company, platoon, section, or file on which a change of formation is based.

Frontage.—The extent of ground covered laterally by troops.

In action (of a machine gun).—A machine gun is said to be in action when it is mounted, loaded, and laid, not necessarily firing.

Incline.—The movement by which ground is gained to the front and flank simultaneously.

Interval.—The lateral space between units on the same alignment.

Interval, deploying.—The lateral space between units in close column or in column, on the same alignment, the space being equal to the frontage of a unit in line.

Line.—Troops formed on the same alignment.

Mass.—A battalion with its companies in line of close columns of platoons, with five paces interval between companies and seven paces distance be.ween platoons.

Mass, open.—A battalion with its companies in line of columns of platoons, with five paces interval between companies.

Masses, column of.—Battalions in mass, on parallel and successive alignments, with any named distance between battalions.

Masses, line of.—A line of battalions in mass, with 10 paces interval between the battalions.

Patrol.—A body of men sent out to reconnoitre or to guard against surprise.

Pivot flank.—The flank on which a unit pivots when changing front.

Pivot guide.—A guide on the pivot flank of a unit.

Position, change of.—A movement by which a body of troops takes up a new alignment.

Ranges, terms applied to.—

Terms applied to ranges.	Rifle.	Field Art.	Heavy Batteries.
	Yards.	Yards.	Yards.
Distant	2,800 to 2,000	6,500 to 5,000	10,000 to 6,500
Long	2,000 to 1,40·¹	5,000 to 4,000	6,500 to 5,000
Effective	1,400 to 600	4,000 to 2,500	5,000 to 2,500
Close	600 and under	2,500 and under	2,500 and under

Rank.—A line of men, side by side.

Squad.—A small body of men formed for recruits' drill.

Supernumeraries.—The non-commissioned officers, &c., forming the third rank.

Wheeling.—A movement by which a body of troops brings forward a flank on a fixed or moving pivot.

INFANTRY TRAINING, 1914.

PART I.—TRAINING.

CHAPTER I.

PRINCIPLES AND SYSTEM OF TRAINING.

PRINCIPLES OF TRAINING.

1. *General instructions.*

1. The object to be aimed at in the training of the infantry soldier is to make him, mentally and physically, a better man than his adversary on the field of battle.

2. The principles on which all training must be based are contained in Field Service Regulations, Part I, and amplified with regard to infantry in Part II of this manual.

3. The preliminary steps necessary for the efficient training of the soldier are :—

    (i) The development of a soldierly spirit.
    (ii) The training of the body.
    (iii) Training in the use of rifle, bayonet, and spade.

After satisfactory progress in these essentials has been made, the soldier must be taught how he can apply what he has learnt to the varied conditions which will confront him in war.

4. The objects in view in developing a soldierly spirit are to help the soldier to bear fatigue, privation, and danger cheerfully ; to imbue him with a sense of honour ; to give him confidence in his superiors and comrades ; to increase his powers of initiative, of self-confidence, and of self-restraint ; to train him to obey orders, or to act in the absence of orders for the advantage of his regiment under all conditions ; to produce such a high degree of courage and disregard of self, that in the stress of battle he will use his brains and his weapons coolly and to the best advantage ; to impress upon him that, so long as he is physically capable of fighting, surrender to the enemy is a disgraceful act ; and finally to teach him how to act in combination with his comrades in order to defeat the enemy. As soon as the recruit joins he should be brought under influences which will tend to produce and increase such a spirit, and it is the duty of all officers and non-commissioned officers to assist in the attainment of this object by their conversation and example.

5. The soldier should be instructed in the deeds which have made the British Army and his regiment famous, and, as his intelligence develops, this instruction should be extended to simple lessons, drawn from military history in general, illustrating how success depends on the above qualities.

The privileges which he inherits as a citizen of a great Empire should be explained to him, and he should be taught to appreciate the honour which is his, as a soldier, of serving his King and country.

6. Drill in close order is of first importance in producing discipline, cohesion, and the habits of absolute and instant obedience to the orders of a superior.

7. The object of the training of the body is to develop in the soldier a capacity for resisting fatigue and privation.

The courses of physical training are laid down in the Manual of Physical Training ; these courses are supplemented by the other training which the soldier receives as a recruit and in the subsequent period of his service.

8. Manly games are of value ; especially if such games and competitions are so arranged that all, and not only selected teams, take their part. Games and competitions should be used to impress the value of combination as well as of individual prowess.

9. The musketry instruction of the soldier is laid down in Musketry Regulations, Part I. Instruction in Bayonet-Fighting is contained in Appendix I of this manual. Instruction in the use of the spade, and in such elementary field engineering as the infantryman is required to know, is contained in the Manual of Field Engineering.

10. The soldier should be made to understand at all periods of his training how the various parts of his course of instruction fit him for his duties in war. In particular, the close connection between musketry and manœuvre must be emphasised.

2. *Responsibility for training.*

1. All commanders, from platoon commanders upwards, are responsible for the training of their commands.

2. Superiors, while delegating authority for the training of subordinate units, are themselves responsible that the training is carried out in accordance with the instructions contained in this manual. They must therefore never forgo their functions of guidance and control, but must exercise a

continuous supervision over the work of their subordinate commanders. The lower the unit being supervised, or the less experienced its leader, the closer must the supervision be. In carrying out this duty, however, officers must act as directors of instruction rather than as instructors. The development of initiative in all subordinate commanders is of vital importance, and anything likely to tend to its suppression must be avoided.

3. The battalion commander is not only responsible for the training of his unit as a whole, but also that the instruction of his officers is conducted in such a way as to fit them for their duties both in war and peace. He will see that the numbers and efficiency of the officers, non-commissioned officers, and men required for special duties are maintained in accordance with the regulations. He will also arrange for such training of the recruit as cannot be carried out at the depôt.

4. The company is the principal training unit in the battalion, and it is essential that it should be regarded as a self-contained unit.

The company commander will arrange for the continuous training of his company throughout the year. He is responsible, not only that his platoon and section commanders are well trained, but also that there is a capable subordinate to take the place of each leader if the necessity should arise.

5. The section commander must know his men thoroughly, and be responsible generally for their discipline and efficiency.

6. The battalion machine-gun officer is responsible for the training of the machine-gun section.

SYSTEM OF TRAINING.

3. *General instructions.*

1. So far as the conditions of enlistment allow, the training, both of the individual and unit, will be progressive and continuous.

The general principle to be observed is first to give the individual a thorough knowledge of his duties and then to teach him to act in combination with his comrades.

2. The training of the infantry soldier is divided into :—

    i. Preliminary, or recruit, training.

    ii. Annual training.

3. The training of the regular and special reserve recruit will be similar. As far as the difference in their conditions of service admit, the training of line and special reserve recruits will be carried out concurrently, and these two classes of recruits should be included in the same squads for instruction. The training should not last more than six months in the case of a regular recruit, and four months, including any training carried out under paragraph 272, Special Reserve Regulations, in the case of a recruit for the special reserve (*see* syllabus in Appendix II), at the end of which period the recruit should be fit in all respects, except musketry, to perform the duties of a trained soldier in the branch of the service to which he belongs.

The training of a recruit for an extra reserve battalion will be in accordance with the syllabus issued with Army Order 299 of 1911.

4. As a general rule the training of recruits should be begun and completed at the regimental depôt. In the case of

special reserve recruits a portion of the training may be performed with special reserve battalions under paragraph 272 Special Reserve Regulations.

5. If, owing to insufficient accommodation at the depôt, line recruits have to be sent to their battalions before completing the course of training, a detailed statement on Army Form, B 2091, showing where they have arrived in the syllabus, should accompany them, and their instruction should be carried on from that point when they join their battalion. The total period of their training with the depôt and battalion should in no case exceed six months without the sanction of the district or brigade commander (*see* Sec. 4. 2). On joining their battalion, such recruits will, for purposes of administration, be posted to companies as supernumerary to the establishment of platoons, but will not be taken for drill, training, or manœuvres with their companies until dismissed recruit training (with the exception of Table A).

6. The annual training of the soldier must be progressive and continuous. With this object the year will be divided into two periods, devoted respectively to —

(i) Individual Training.
(ii) Collective Training.

The object of individual training is to prepare the individual officer, non-commissioned officer, or soldier for the duties which he will be required to carry out in war. Particular attention will be paid during this period to the training of junior officers and non-commissioned officers with a view to their becoming efficient instructors.

The object of collective training is to render sections, platoons, companies, and the larger units and formations capable of manœuvre and co-operation in battle.

7. The instruction of individuals and units is not to be considered as limited to the periods allotted for individual and collective training. Advantage must be taken of any opportunities which may arise for individual training during the period of collective training, and *vice versa*.

8. It is undesirable to define exactly how the time available for the various courses of training is to be employed. Commanders must design for themselves programmes of training, which will ensure that the required standard of efficiency is reached within the time allotted.

9. The success or failure of each year's collective training will largely depend upon the care and attention devoted to the individual training which precedes it.

10. It is important that leave and furlough should be so arranged that each company will be as complete as possible for a period or periods amounting to one month during the period of individual training, but brigade commanders may give such orders on this point as they deem best for their particular station.

11. Collective training should begin with the training of the section, and continue with that of the platoon, company, and larger units in succession.

12. The annual training of units of the Special Reserve and Territorial Force infantry should be carried out on the same principles as have been laid down for the Regular Forces.

It is suggested that the training of the infantry of the Forces of the Overseas Dominions should also be conducted on similar lines.

13. It is not possible for the Special Reserve and Territorial Force infantry, in the limited time for training at their disposal, to carry out the whole course, but the spirit of the

instructions should be observed. Their annual training in camp should be principally devoted to company training.

4. *Recruit training.*

1. The course of recruit training should include :—
    i. The development of a soldierly spirit.
    ii. Instruction in barrack and camp duties, cleanliness, care of feet, smartness, orders, and such regulations as immediately affect the soldier.
    iii, Physical training, under qualified instructors, as laid down in the Manual of Physical Training.
    iv. Infantry Training, Chapters II to V inclusive.
    v. Marching, march discipline, and running.
    vi. Musketry instruction under the following heads :—
        (*a*) General description of the rifle and ammunition used.
        (*b*) Instruction in care of arms.
        (*c*) Elementary instruction in the theory of rifle fire.
        (*d*) Aiming and firing.
        (*e*) Visual training and judging distance.
    vii. Movements at night, and practice in using the ears and eyes at night (Sec. 113).
    viii. Guards and outposts.
    ix. Rudiments of the duties of a soldier in the field.
    x. Use of the entrenching implement and entrenching tools.
    (xi) Bayonet fighting.

2. Before being dismissed recruit training every regular recruit will be examined by the depôt or battalion commander and a medical officer, who will determine whether he has

attained the necessary standard of efficiency (*see* paragraph 3) and is physically fit for the duties of a trained soldier.

This examination may take place as soon as it is thought that a batch of recruits has attained the required standard, but never later than six months after enlistment, deducting any periods spent in hospital or under detention.

When once a recruit has been passed as above, he must be considered a trained man with the exception of musketry. A recruit must on no account be passed temporarily and the final stages of the syllabus postponed with a view to taking him for other duties in the meanwhile. The entire course of his recruit training (including Table A, if possible, *see* para. 10) must be continuous.

A special report must be made by the depôt or battalion commander, to the district or brigade commander as the case may be, about any line recruit who, after six months training, is found too weak or too awkward for the duties of a trained soldier.

3. The necessary standard of efficiency before a regular recruit is dismissed recruit training is as follows :—

(*a*) The recruit must be able to turn out correctly in marching order and fit to take his place in the ranks of his company in close and extended order drill.

(*b*) Carry out an ordinary route march in marching order.

(*c*) Have completed his recruit gymnastic training.

(*d*) Be sufficiently instructed in musketry and visual training to commence a recruit's course of musketry immediately after being dismissed recruit training.

(e) Be sufficiently trained to take part in night operations.

(f) Understand the principles of protection and his duties on guard or outpost.

(g) Be able to use the entrenching implement and entrenching tools and understand the method of carrying tools.

(h) Be well grounded in bayonet fighting.

4. Recruits will be formed in squads for instructional purposes. The number of men in each squad should be as small as the number of available instructors will allow.

5. Squad instructors will be most carefully selected. They must be intelligent, energetic, smart in their bearing, and thoroughly well trained in the art of instruction. It will usually be advantageous for the instructor to remain with the same squad throughout the period of training and carry out the whole of the instruction except physical training, which will be taught only by fully qualified instructors.

6. The course of instruction should be so arranged as to begin with about 20 hours work per week, gradually increasing to about 28 hours work per week. The daily work should be arranged with as much variety as possible, and must be suited to the aptitude of the individual recruit. Every endeavour must be made to avoid monotony, with its consequent loss of interest.

7. A syllabus for a course of six months' training is given in the Appendix to assist officers charged with the training of recruits in framing their programmes. This syllabus, which is published as a guide only, and need not be rigidly followed, is so arranged as to admit of recruits who show special aptitude being dismissed their recruit training at the end of

the twentieth week.   In addition to the work mentioned in this syllabus recruits must be given practical instruction in laying out kits, the repair of clothing, and the cleaning of clothing and equipment.

8. Equipment will be issued on joining, but, with the exception of waistbelt and cartridge carriers, which will be used for all musketry parades after the first fortnight, it will not be worn on parade during the first month.   Instructors will wear waistbelts on all parades, with cartridge carriers on musketry parades.

Dummy cartridges will be used by both instructors and recruits on all musketry parades.

9. Rifles will be issued when the depôt or battalion commander directs, but not earlier than the second week.

10. As soon as possible after being dismissed recruit training young soldiers will be put through Table A.   Until this course is begun they will be given five hours a week special musketry instruction.

5. *Annual individual training.*

1. Annual individual training will consist of—

    i. The training of officers in professional duties (*see* King's Regulations and Training and Manœuvre Regulations).

    ii. The training of non-commissioned officers and privates likely to become non-commissioned officers in the duties of a section commander, in fire direction and control, use of ground, map reading, reconnaissance, reports, wood and village fighting, outpost work, and the conduct of infantry patrols (*see also* Training and Manœuvre Regulations, Sec. **38**).   This instruction will be carried out in the company, battalion classes being reserved for special subjects outside the ordinary routine of training.

iii. The training of soldiers in their individual duties in the section in war, including drill in close and extended order, fire discipline, duties on outpost, finding their way across country in the dark, knotting and lashing, and the uses of the various forms of spars. Instruction in the use of the entrenching implement and entrenching tools should be continued, men being taught the general principles of the siting of trenches, the construction of overhead cover, and the circumstances in which trenches are required. Lectures should be given during this period with the object of developing a sense of personal honour, duty, patriotism, and *esprit de corps*.

iv. Practice for all ranks in visual training, in judging distance, and in aiming under varied conditions ; the improvement of indifferent shots, and practice on the miniature and open ranges.

v. Physical training. Every man should be exercised in the trained soldier's physical exercises as laid down in the Manual of Physical Training, and should be practised out of doors in marching, running, and surmounting obstacles.

vi. Bayonet fighting (*see* Appendix I).

vii. Training in packing and loading all available descriptions of transport and, where facilities exist or can be improvised, in the embarkation, disembarkation, entraining and detraining of animals and vehicles.

viii. Training of specialists.

2. At the beginning of the period of individual training

battalion and company signallers, machine gun detachments, range takers, and transport drivers will be brought up to establishment and their training will be begun. Extra men will also be trained to replace casualties caused by drafts, transfers to the reserve, &c. The individual training period is the most convenient time for specialist training, and full use should be made of it for this purpose.

6. *The annual training of the section and platoon.*

1. The company commander will allot such time as he considers desirable at the beginning of his course of company training in field operations (*see* Sec. 7) for the training of his sections and platoons (*see* Chapter VIII). The training of the section borders so nearly on the training of the individual that it may be possible to complete it during the period allotted to individual training.

2. All non-commissioned officers and men of the section or platoon, except those mentioned in Sec. 7, para. 3, must be present for this training.

3. Platoon commanders will prepare a programme of work to be carried out during the period allotted for section and platoon training.

4. Success in battle will largely depend on the efficiency of fire-unit commanders. The normal fire-unit will be the section. The practical training of all section commanders in handling their sections is therefore of supreme importance, and, with this object, every section should be regarded as a distinct unit and should be commanded throughout its training by its own leader. When, however, the strength of a section falls below 5 men (including the leader), it may be joined temporarily to another section for work in the field. **But in all circumstances platoon and company commanders are**

responsible that all four section commanders in the platoon are given such practice in command as will make them efficient fire-unit commanders.

7. *The annual training of the company.*

1. During the first months of the collective training period each company will be struck off all duties for a special course of training in field operations (*see* Chapter VIII), and for the annual course of musketry.

2. The personnel of battalion headquarters, with the exception of those excused in the next paragraph, will perform company training and will be temporarily attached to sections for this purpose. It is at the discretion of the battalion commander whether these details are trained with the companies to which they are allotted for administration or otherwise.

3. The following will be exempted from the training of the company in field operations : Battalion signallers who have completed three company trainings in the ranks, bandsmen, the machine-gun section, and those exempted from the annual course of musketry. Private soldiers of more than 15 years' service, who are specially employed, may be exempted with the concurrence of the battalion commander. Every other officer, non-commissioned officer, and man will be trained, and will be relieved of other duties for this purpose.

8. *The annual training of machine-gun sections.*

1. The two non-commissioned officers and twelve privates shown in the establishment* of a machine-gun section will be trained as the battalion machine-gun section. Two

---

* In India, owing to pack transport, four privates from the reserve section are added as mule holders.

non-commissioned officers and twelve men in addition will be trained, as opportunity offers, to replace casualties.

2. A subaltern officer, other than the assistant adjutant, will be selected in each battalion to command and train the machine-gun section, under the orders of the battalion commander. In each brigade an officer, who is not the machine-gun officer of one of the battalions of the brigade, will be selected to supervise the firing practice and to conduct the brigade training of machine-gun sections.

3. Soldiers selected for duty with a machine-gun section should possess, as far as possible, the following qualifications :—good physique, good eye-sight, calm temperament, fair education, and mechanical aptitude.

4. It is most important that men selected for the machine-gun section should remain with it as long as possible in order that they may acquire a high standard of skill. Young soldiers of about a year's service are therefore the most suitable for selection. The officer, non-commissioned officers, and men of the machine-gun section will fire the range practices prescribed for the rifle in the Musketry Regulations, Part I, with one of the companies of the battalion. The classification of detachments will be determined by battalion commanders after the annual machine-gun course. This paragraph applies also to special reserve battalions, whether the machine-gun sections belong to the battalion or are detailed for armament coast defence guns, except that machine gunners of such battalions will not be classified.

5. Details as to the care and mechanism of the gun are contained in the handbook of the gun. Instructions as to the course of firing are contained in the Musketry Regulations, Part I.

6. The elementary training, which may be carried out

(B 10984)   B

in the neighbourhood of barracks, will consist of instruction in the mechanism of the gun; in adjusting the tripod, mounting and dismounting the gun; in the drill and methods of laying, ranging, and firing; in packing and unpacking limbered wagons; in filling a belt quickly and correctly; in the use of the range finder; in semaphore signalling, and in the signals for the observation and control of fire.

7. As soon as the men of a section are thoroughly conversant with the mechanism, and have qualified in the tests of elementary training for the machine gun (see Musketry Regulations, Part I), their further training will be carried out, as far as possible, in open country away from barracks. During this training the sections should be practised in bringing the gun into action; in fire discipline; in fire control; in laying and ranging in every variety of country; in utilising natural cover when advancing into action; and in constructing cover from both view and fire. The men should also be trained in range taking, judging distance, and in the use of field glasses.

8. When the section is proficient in these branches of training, the battalion commander will arrange for it to be trained with one or more companies which have reached the more advanced stages of company training, in order that it may be practised in co-operating with other troops and in dealing with such situations as would confront it in war.

9. *The annual training of the battalion.*

1. When all the companies have completed their course of training in field operations, the battalion will be struck off all duties for a course of battalion training.

CHAPTER II.

SQUAD DRILL.

10. *Method of instructing recruits.*

1. The instructor should be clear, firm, concise, and patient ; he must make allowance for the different capacities of the men, and avoid discouraging nervous recruits ; he must remember that much may be taught by personal example, and that careful individual instruction is the best means of developing the intelligence.

2. The instructor will teach as much as possible by demonstration, performing the movements himself or making a smart recruit perform them. The detail for each movement as given in this manual is for the information of instructors, who must avoid repeating it word for word, because such a method is wearisome and monotonous and would not be understood by some recruits.

The instructor will explain the reason for every movement and formation, and its application in the field.

3. Drills will be short and frequent to avoid the exhaustion of the instructor and recruits.

4. Recruits will be advanced progressively from one exercise to another, men of inferior capacity being put back to a less advanced squad.

5. At first the recruit will be placed in position by the

instructor; afterwards he should not be touched, but made to correct his own position when faults are pointed out.

6. When the various motions have been learnt, instruction "by numbers" will cease.

11. Words of command.

1. Commands will be pronounced distinctly, and sufficiently loud to be heard by all concerned.

2. Commands which consist of one word will be preceded by a caution. The caution, or cautionary part of a command, will be given deliberately and distinctly; the last or executive part, which, as a rule, should consist of only one word or syllable, will be given sharply: as Battalion— Halt; Right—Form; Right hand--Salute. A pause will be made between the caution and the executive word. Men will be taught to act upon the last sound of the executive word of command.

3. When the formation is moving, executive words will be completed as the men begin the pace which will bring them to the spot on which the command is to be executed. The caution must be commenced accordingly (see also Sec. 26, 1, note).

4. Young officers and non-commissioned officers will be frequently practised in giving words of command.

5. Indistinct and slovenly words of command beget slovenly movements and must be avoided.

6. The cautions and commands in this manual are, as a rule, given with regard to one flank only, but the same principle applies equally to movements to the other flank, which will also be practised.

SQUAD DRILL WITHOUT ARMS.

SQUAD DRILL WITH INTERVALS.

12. *Formation of squads with intervals.*

1. A few men will be placed in single rank at arm's length apart ; while so formed, they will be termed a *squad with intervals.*

2. Instruction can best be imparted to a squad in single rank, but, if want of space makes it necessary, the squad may consist of two ranks, in which case the men of the rear rank will cover the intervals between the men in the front rank, so that in marching they may take their own points, as directed in Sec. **21,** 4.

3. When recruits have learned to dress as described in Sec. **16,** they will be taught to fall in as above described, and then to dress and correct their intervals. After they have been instructed as far as Sec. **26,** they may fall in as directed in Sec. **27.**

4. Recruits formed into a squad will be directed to observe the relative places they hold with each other ; while resting between the exercises they may be permitted to fall out and move about ; they will be instructed on the command *Fall in,* to fall in as they stood at first.

13. *Attention.**

Squad—Attention.

Spring up to the following position :—

Heels together and in line. Feet turned out at an angle

---

* In this and the following sections the title of the section or of the movement is shown in *italics,* and is followed in the next line by the caution or executive word of command in **thick type.** The body of the section contains the detail. Cautions or words of command referred to in the detail are in *italics.*

of about 45 degrees. Knees straight. Body erect and
carried evenly over the thighs, with the shoulders (which
should be level and square to the front) down and moderately
back—this should bring the chest into its natural forward
position without any straining or stiffening. Arms hanging
easily from the shoulders as straight as the natural bend of
the arm, when the muscles are relaxed, will allow, but with
the thumbs immediately behind the seams of the trousers.
Wrists straight. Palms of the hands turned towards the
thighs, hands partially closed, backs of fingers touching the
thigh lightly, thumb close to forefinger. Neck erect. Head
balanced evenly on the neck, and not poked forward, eyes
looking their own height and straight to the front.

The weight of the body should be balanced on both feet,
and evenly distributed between the fore part of the feet and
the heels.

The breathing must not in any way be restricted, and no
part of the body should be either drawn in or pushed out.

The position is one of readiness, but there should be no
stiffness or unnatural straining to maintain it.

Particular attention should be paid to the heels being in
line, as otherwise the man cannot stand square in the ranks.

14. *Standing at ease.*

Stand at—Ease.

Keeping the legs straight, carry the left foot about twelve
inches to the left so that the weight of the body rests equally
on both feet ; at the same time carry the hands behind
the back and place the back of one hand in the palm of the
other, grasping it lightly with the fingers and thumb, and

allowing the arms to hang easily at their full extent.   (It is immaterial which hand grasps the other.)

Notes.—i. In marching order without the rifle the arms will be retained as in the position of *attention*.

ii. When a recruit falls in for instruction he will *stand at ease* after he has got his dressing.

15. *Standing easy.*

Stand—Easy.

The limbs, head, and body may be moved, but the man will not move from the ground on which he is standing, so that on coming to *attention* there will be no loss of dressing. Slouching attitudes are not permitted.

16. *Dressing a squad with intervals.*

Right—Dress.

Each recruit, except the right-hand man, will turn his head and eyes to the right and will then extend his right arm, back of the hand upwards, finger tips touching the shoulder of the man on his right.   At the same time he will take up his dressing in line by moving, with short quick steps, till he is just able to distinguish the lower part of the face of the second man beyond him.   Care must be taken to carry the body backward or forward with the feet, the shoulders being kept perfectly square in their original position.

Eyes—Front.

The head and eyes will be turned smartly to the front. the arm dropped, and the position of *attention* resumed.

17. *Turning by numbers.*

1. Turning to the Right—One.

Keeping both knees straight and the body erect, turn to

the right on the right heel and left toe, raising the left heel and right toe in doing so.

On the completion of this preliminary movement, the right foot must be flat on the ground and the left heel raised ; both knees straight, and the weight of the body, which must be erect, on the right foot.

Two.

Bring the left heel smartly up to the right without stamping the foot on the ground.

2. Turning to the Left—One.

Turn to the left, as described above, on the left heel and right toe, the weight of the body being on the left foot on the completion of the movement.

Two.

Bring the right heel smartly up to the left without stamping the foot on the ground.

3. Turning About—One.

Keeping both knees straight and the body erect, turn to the right-about on the right heel and left toe, raising the left heel and right toe in doing so.

On the completion of this preliminary movement, the right foot must be flat on the ground and the left heel raised ; both knees straight, and the weight of the body, which must be erect, on the right foot.

Two.

Bring the left heel smartly up to the right without stamping the foot on the ground.

PLATE I.

4. Inclining to the Right—One.

As described for turning to the right, but turning only half right.

Two.

As described for turning to the right.

5. Inclining to the Left—One.

As described for turning to the left, but turning only half left.

Two.

As described for turning to the left.

Note.—In turning " judging the time " commands are *Right* (or *left* or *about*) *Turn, Right* (or *left*) *Incline* ; the movements described above will be carried out on the word *Turn* or *Incline,* observing the two distinct motions.

18. *Saluting to the front.*

1. *By numbers.*

Salute by Numbers—One.

Bring the right hand smartly, with a circular motion, to the head, palm to the front, fingers extended and close together, point of the forefinger 1 inch above the right eye, or touching edge of peak of cap just above right eyebrow as in illustration, thumb close to the forefinger ; elbow in line, and nearly square, with the shoulder (*see* Plate I).

Two.

Cut away the arm smartly to the side.

2. *Judging the time.*

Salute, Judging the Time—Salute.

Go through the motions as in para. 1, and, after a pause equal to two paces in quick time, cut away the arm.

Notes.—i. Saluting to the side (Plate II), is carried out as in Sec. **18**, on the command *right (or left) hand salute*, except that, as the hand is brought to the salute, the head will be turned towards the person saluted. The salute will be made with the hand further from the person saluted.

ii. Recruits will be practised in marching two or three together, saluting points being placed on either side. When several men are together, the man nearest to the point will give the time.

iii. When a soldier passes an officer he will salute on the third pace before reaching him, and lower the hand on the third pace after passing him; if carrying a cane he will place it smartly under the disengaged arm, cutting away the hand before saluting.

iv. A soldier, if sitting when an officer approaches, will stand at attention, facing the officer, and salute with the right hand; if two or more men are sitting or standing about, the senior non-commissioned officer or oldest soldier will face the officer, call the whole to attention, and alone will salute (as above).

v. When a soldier addresses an officer he will halt two paces from him, and salute with the right hand. He will also salute before withdrawing.

vi. When appearing before an officer in a room, he will salute without removing his cap.

vii. A soldier without his cap, or when carrying anything other than his arms, will, if standing still, come to attention

PLATE II.   *To face p. 24.*

as an officer passes ; if walking, he will turn his head smartly towards the officer in passing him.

viii. A soldier, when riding a bicycle or driving a motor vehicle, will turn his head smartly towards an officer in passing him, and will not move his hands from the handle bar or steering wheel.

ix. A soldier driving a horsed vehicle will bring his whip to a perpendicular position, with the right hand resting on the thigh, and turn his head smartly towards an officer when passing him.

x. A soldier riding on a vehicle will turn his head smartly towards an officer when passing him.

xi. Warrant and non-commissioned officers when wearing a sword will salute with the right hand.

xii. The term " officer " includes naval officers, certain naval warrant officers* and military and naval officers of foreign powers (*see* King's Regulations, paras. 1763 and 1788).

xiii. Officers† or soldiers passing troops with uncased standards or colours will salute the standard or colours and the commanding officer (if senior).

xiv. Officers and soldiers passing a military funeral will salute the body.

xv. When in command of unarmed parties, officers, and warrant and non-commissioned officers wearing a sword, will, in paying or returning a compliment, give the command *Eyes right* (or *left*) and at the same time salute with the right hand.

---

* Chief gunners, chief boatswains, chief carpenters, chief artificer engineers, and chief schoolmasters in the Royal Navy rank as 2nd lieutenants in the Army, and will be saluted by warrant officers, N.C.Os. and men.
† Instructions for saluting with the sword for officers are contained in " Ceremonial."

Ranks other than officers, when not wearing a sword, will similarly give the command *Eyes right* (or *left*), but will salute with the hand farthest away from the person saluted.

19. *Length of pace, and time in marching.*

1. *Length of pace.*—In *slow* and in *quick time* the length of a pace is 30 inches. In *stepping out*, it is 33 inches, in *double time*, 40, in *stepping short*, 21, and in the *side pace,* 14 inches.

When a soldier takes a side pace to clear or cover another, as in forming fours, Sec. **43**, the pace will be 27 inches.

2. *Time.*—In *slow time*, 75 paces are taken in a minute. In *quick time*, 120 paces, equal to 100 yards in a minute, or 3 miles 720 yards in an hour, are taken. Except during the first weeks of recruit training, recruits, when not in marching order, will take 140 paces per minute in *quick time* at drill. In *double time*, 180 paces, equal to 200 yards a minute, are taken. The time of the *side pace* is the same as for the *quick step.*

Marching in *slow time* will be practised only in the early stages of recruit training, and when required for ceremonial purposes, *see* " Ceremonial."

Distances of 100 and 200 yards will be marked on the drill ground, and non-commissioned officers and men practised in keeping correct time and length of pace.

20. *The drum and pace stick.*

1. Recruits are not to be taught to march without the constant use of the drum and pace stick.

2. Before the squad is put in motion a drummer will beat the time in which the men are to march, the men paying careful attention. The squad will then be marched off, and

the drummer will beat the time occasionally while the men are on the move.

3. In order to ascertain whether the time is beaten correctly, a pendulum should be used.

4. The length of the pace in marching will be corrected with the pace stick, the accuracy of which should occasionally be tested by measurement.

21. *Position in marching.*

1. In marching, the soldier will maintain the position of the head and body as directed in Sec. **13.**   He must be well balanced on his limbs.   In slow time his arms and hands must be kept steady by his sides.   In quick time the arms should swing naturally from the shoulder, the right arm swinging forward with the left leg, and the left arm with the right leg.   The movement of the leg must spring from the haunch and be free and natural.

2. The legs should be swung forward freely and naturally from the hip joints, each leg as it swings forward being bent sufficiently at the knee to enable the foot to clear the ground.   The foot should be carried straight to the front, and, without being drawn back, placed firmly upon the ground with the knee straight, but so as not to jerk the body.

3. Although several recruits may be drilled together in a squad with intervals, they must act independently, precisely as if they were being instructed singly.   They will thus learn to march in a straight line, and to take a correct pace, both as regards length and time, without reference to the other men of the squad.

4. Before the squad is put in motion, the instructor will take care that each man is square to the front and in correct line with the remainder.   The recruit will be taught to take

a point straight to his front, by fixing his eyes upon some distant object, and then observing some nearer point in the same straight line, such as a stone, tuft of grass, or other object. The same procedure will be followed by the man on the named flank or by the named number, when marching in other formations (*see* Sec. **31**).

22. *Marching in quick time.*

1. *The quick march.*

Quick—March.

The squad will step off together with the left foot, in quick time, observing the rules in Sec. **21.**

Note.—For the first week of recruit training it is recommended that all squad drill should be with intervals and in slow time only. The executive word of command will be *Slow— March.* The men will step off and march as described for Quick—March, but in slow time, and keeping the arms and hands steady at the sides, pointing the toes downward and placing them on the ground before the heel, each leg being straightened smartly as it comes to the front before the foot is placed on the ground.

2. *The halt.*

Squad—Halt.

The moving foot will complete its pace, and the other will be brought smartly up in line with it, without stamping.

3. *Stepping out.*

Step—Out.

The moving foot will complete its pace, and the soldier

will lengthen the pace by 3 inches, leaning forward a little, but without altering the time.

Note.—This step is used when a slight increase of speed, without an alteration of time, is required ; on the command *Quick—March* the usual pace will be resumed.

4. *Stepping short.*
Step—Short.
The foot advancing will complete its pace, after which the pace will be shortened by 9 inches until the command *Quick— March* is given, when the quick step will be resumed.

5. *Marking time.*
Mark—Time.
The foot then advancing will complete its pace, after which the time will be continued, without advancing, by raising each foot alternately about 6 inches, keeping the feet almost parallel with the ground, the knees raised to the front, the arms steady at the sides, and the body steady. On the command *Forward,* the pace at which the men were moving will be resumed.

6. *Stepping back from the halt.*
—— **Paces Step Back—March.**
Step back the named number of paces of 30 inches straight to the rear, commencing with the left foot, observing the rules in Sec. **21.**

Note.—Stepping back should not exceed four paces.

23. *Changing step.*

1. *When on the march.*
Change—Step.
The advancing foot will complete its pace, and the ball

of the rear foot will be brought up to the heel of the advanced one, which will make another step forward, so that the time will not be lost, two successive steps being taken with the same foot.

2. *When marking time.*
Change—Step.

Make two successive beats with the same foot.

24. *Marching in double time.*

1. *The double march.*
Double—March.

Step off with the left foot and double on the toes with easy swinging strides, inclining the body slightly forward, but maintaining its correct carriage. The feet must be picked up cleanly from the ground at each pace, and the thigh, knee, and ankle joints must all work freely and without stiffness. The whole body should be carried forward by a thrust from the rear foot without unnecessary effort. The heels must not be raised towards the seat, but the foot carried straight to the front and the toes placed lightly on the ground. The arms should swing easily from the shoulders and should be bent at the elbow, the forearm forming an angle of about 135 degrees with the upper arm (*i.e.*, midway between a straight arm and a right angle at the elbow), fists clenched, backs of the hands outward, and the arms swung sufficiently clear of the body to allow of full freedom for the chest. The shoulders should be kept steady and square to the front and the head erect.

2. *The halt.*
Squad—Halt.

As in Sec. **22,** 2, at the same time dropping the hands to the position of *attention*.

3. *Marking time.*

Mark—Time.

Act as in Sec. **22, 5,** the arms and hands being carried as when marching in double time, but with the swing of the arms reduced.

25. *The side step.*

1. Right (*or* Left) Close—March, *or*—**Paces Right (*or* Left) Close—March.**

Each man will carry his right foot 14 inches direct to the right, and instantly close his left foot to it, thus completing the pace ; he will proceed to take the next pace in the same manner. Shoulders to be kept square, knees straight, unless on rough or broken ground. The direction must be kept in a straight line to the flank.

2. *The halt.*

Squad—Halt.

On the command *Halt,* which will be given when the number of paces has not been specified, the men will complete the pace they are taking, and remain steady.

Note.—Soldiers should not usually be moved to a flank by the side step more than 12 paces.

26. *Turning when on the march.*

1. Right—Turn.

Each man will turn in the named direction, and move on at once without checking his pace.

Note.—A soldier will always turn to the right on the left foot ; and to the left on the right foot. The word *turn* will be given as the foot on which the turn is to be made is coming to the ground ; if it is not so given, the soldier will move on one pace and then turn.

2. About—Turn.

The soldier will turn right-about on his own ground in three beats of the time in which he is marching. Having completed the turn about the soldier will at once move forward, the fourth pace being a full pace.

3. Right—Incline.

On the word *Incline*, make a half-turn in the required direction.

SQUAD DRILL IN SINGLE RANK.

27. *Formation of squads in single rank.*

Recruits will at this stage be formed in single rank without intervals, each man occupying a lateral space of 27 inches. Thus ten men occupy nine paces. The accuracy of the spaces should be frequently tested. Squads will fall in and dress by the right unless otherwise ordered.

28. *Dressing in single rank.*

Right—Dress (*after the word Halt only*).

In all cases, except after the word *Halt* and at ceremonial drill, a soldier will take up his own dressing without orders. After the word *Halt*, a soldier will stand steady. If it be necessary to correct the dressing, the command *Right* (*or left*)—*Dress* will be given. Each man, except the man on the named flank, will then look towards the flank by which he is to dress with a smart turn of the head and, commencing with the man nearest the flank by which the dressing is made, will move up or back to his place successively. Each man will look to his front as soon as he has got his dressing (*see* Sec. **16**).

Men will only be dressed after the word *Halt* when a correction of the alignment is necessary.

29. *Numbering a squad.*

Squad—Number.

The squad will number off from the right, the right-hand man calling out " *One,*" the next on his left " *Two,*" and so on.

30. *Opening and closing a squad.*

1. Open Ranks—March.

The odd numbers will take two paces forward; when the paces are completed the men who have moved (except the right-hand man of each rank) will look to the right and correct the dressing quickly, looking to the front as soon as the dressing is correct.

2. Re-form Ranks—March.

The odd numbers will step back two paces; when the paces are completed the squad will dress without orders, as in Sec. 28.

31. *Marching in single rank.*

1. By the Right (*or* Left *or* by No. —), Quick—March.

As in Sec. **22.** Each man will preserve his position in the general line by an occasional glance towards the directing man, who will act as in Sec. **21, 4.**

2. By the Right (*or* Left *or* by No. —), Double—March.

As in para. 1 above, but in double time.

32. *Changing the pace from quick to double time, and vice versa.*

1. Double—March.

Complete the next pace in quick time and then continue in double time as in Sec. 24.

2. Quick—March.

Complete the next pace in double time and then break into quick time, dropping the arms to their usual position.

33. *The diagonal march* (Plate III, fig. 1).

Right—Incline.

Each man will make a half turn in the required direction and, if on the march, will move diagonally in that direction.

34. *Changing direction* (Plate III, fig. 2).

Right—Form.

The right-hand man will make a full turn in the required direction, and the remainder a half turn.

Quick—March.

The right-hand man will mark time and the remainder will mark time when they come up into the new alignment.

Note.—Should the squad be required to halt on reaching the new alignment the command will be preceded by the caution *At the Halt* ; each man will then halt and take up his dressing on reaching the new alignment. If the squad is on the move the command *Quick March* is omitted.

PLATE III.   *To face p.* 34.

THE DIAGONAL MARCH.

Fig. 1.
Right Incline.

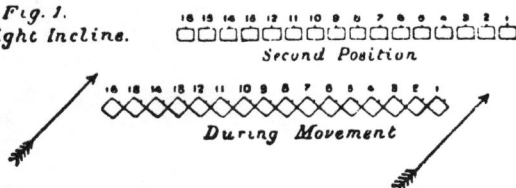

Second Position

During Movement

First Position

Fig. 2.
Changing Direction.
At the Halt. Right form.

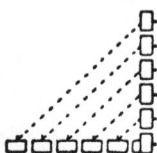

Fig 3
Forming up.
On the Left Form Squad

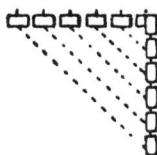

Forward.

The squad will move forward in the new direction.

Note.—Forming at any angle will be practised. If necessary, the first three men may be dressed at the required angle and the remainder be ordered to form upon them.

35. *Marching as in file.*

1. *From the halt.*

Right—Turn.

As in Sec. **17.** The men will now cover each other exactly. The head of the man immediately in front of each soldier, when he is correctly covered, will conceal the heads of all the others in front of him.

Quick—March.

The whole will step off, without increasing or diminishing the distance between each other.

Note.—This will also be practised on the move, the words *Quick March* being omitted.

2. *Changing direction.*

Right—Wheel.

The leading man will move round a quarter of the circumference of a circle having a radius of 4 feet. The other men, in succession, will follow in his footsteps without increasing or diminishing their distances from each other or altering the time, but shortening the pace a little with the inner foot.

3. Rear Files—Cover.

If the squad is halted or ordered to *Mark Time* when only

a part of the men have wheeled into the new direction, the men who have not yet wheeled will cover off on those who have, moving to their places by the shortest route.

4. *Forming squad on the move* (Plate III, fig. 3).

On the Left, Form—Squad.

The leading man will mark time, the remainder will make a partial turn in the named direction and form upon him, marking time as they come into the line.

Forward.

The squad will move on in line in the direction in which it was originally marching in file.

Note.—After forming squad on the right, the left will normally be ordered to direct.

5. *Forming squad at the halt.*

At the Halt, on the Left, Form—Squad.

The leading man will halt, the remainder will make a partial turn in the named direction and form upon him, halting and dressing as they come into the line.

SQUAD DRILL IN TWO RANKS.

36. *Formation of a squad in two ranks.*

The squad will now be formed for drill in two ranks. The men will take their places in succession, commencing from the right unless they are ordered to form on the other flank, each occupying a lateral space of 27 inches. Each man of the rear rank will be placed 60 inches from the man in front of him, measuring from heel to heel, and will cover him correctly, the two men thus placed forming a *file*. When the squad consists of an uneven number of men the third man from the left of the front rank will be a *blank* (or incomplete) *file* ; that is, he will have no rear rank man. Squads will dress by the right unless otherwise ordered. The instructions for dressing by the right in the following sections may be varied so as to apply to dressing by the left.

37. *Dressing.*

Right—Dress (*after the word Halt only*).

In all cases, except after the word *Halt* and at ceremonial drill, a soldier will take up his own dressing without orders. After the word *Halt* a soldier will stand steady. If it is necessary to correct the dressing, the command *Right* (or *Left*)— *Dress* will be given. Each man of both the front and rear ranks, except the right (or left) file, will look towards the right (or left) with a smart turn of the head, and will move up or back to his place successively commencing with the file nearest the right (or left) file. Rear rank men must also correctly cover their front rank men. Each man will look to his front as soon as he has got his dressing.

38. *Numbering a squad.*

Squad—Number.

The men of the front rank will number off smartly as in Sec. **29**. Each rear rank man will listen to the number given by his front rank man, which number will also be his own.

39. *Opening and closing a squad.*

Open Ranks—March.

The odd numbers of the front rank will step forward two paces, the even numbers of the rear rank will step back

two paces ; as soon as the paces are completed, the men
who have moved (except the right-hand man of each of the
four ranks) will look to the right and correct the dressing
quickly, looking to the front as soon as the dressing is
correct.

Re-form Ranks—March.

The odd numbers of the front rank will step back two
paces, the even numbers of the rear rank will step forward
two paces, and, as soon as the paces are completed, the
squad will dress by the right, without word of command.

40. *Marching in line.*

By the Right (*or* Left), Quick (*or* Double)—March.

The whole will step off, the front rank man of the file
on the named flank taking a point to march on. The men
of each rank, except the directing file, will glance occasionally
to the named flank to maintain their dressing. The men
of the rear rank will also preserve their covering and distance
from the front rank.

If there is a blank file, he will always be with the front
rank ; when the squad is turned about on the march he will
step out to gain his place in the new front rank ; if the
squad is turned about at the halt he will take two paces
forward after turning about.

Note.—When a squad turns about the ranks are thereby
changed, and the former rear rank becomes the front rank ;
the former front rank the rear rank.

When, however, the squad is required to fall back for a
short distance only before resuming the original direction,
ranks will not be changed. In this case the command will

be *The Squad will Retire, About—Turn*, and on completion, *The Squad will Advance, About —Turn*.

2. *The diagonal march.*

Right—Incline.

As in Sec. **33.** The men of the rear rank will preserve their relative positions with the men of the front rank, in order that they may cover correctly when they are again turned into line.

3. *Changing direction.*

Right—Form.

The right-hand man of the front rank will make a full turn in the required direction and the remainder of the front rank a partial turn. The rear rank will stand fast.

Quick—March.

The right-hand man of the front rank will mark time; the remainder will step off, the men of the rear rank conforming to the movements of their front rank men. The whole will mark time when they come into their places in the new alignment.

Forward.

The whole will move off in the new direction.

Notes.—1. If the squad is on the march the command *Quick—March* is omitted.

2. If required to halt after forming, the command will be *At the Halt—Right Form.* The right-hand man, after turning to the right, will stand fast instead of marking time and the remainder will halt and dress as they come up.

3. Squads may be formed half or quarter right or left, on the command *Half (or quarter) Right (or left)—Form.*

41. *Marching in file.*

1. *Turning into file.*

Right—Turn.

The whole will turn to the right (or left), and lead on in that direction without checking the pace. The men of the rear rank will dress by their front rank men.

2. *Changing direction.*

Right—Wheel.

The inner man of the leading file will move round a quarter of the circumference of a circle having a radius of 4 feet, stepping short to enable the outer man of the file to wheel with him. When the quarter circle is completed, the file leads on in the new direction. The other files in succession will follow in the footsteps of the leading file without increasing or diminishing their distances from each other or altering the time.

Note.—If the squad is halted, or ordered to mark time, when only a part of it has wheeled into the new direction, the remainder will cover off as directed in Sec. **35**, 3, on the command *Rear Files—Cover.*

3. *Forming squad.*

On the Left (*or* Right), Form—Squad.

The left-hand man of the leading file, if the formation is on the left (or the right-hand man of the leading file, if the formation is on the right), will mark time.

The remainder will make a partial turn in the named

direction and form upon him, marking time as they come into the alignment.

Forward.

The squad will move on in line in the direction in which it was originally marching in file.

Notes.—i. After forming squad on the right, the left will normally be ordered to direct.

ii. If desired to halt on completion, the command will be *At the Halt, on the Left (or right), Form—Squad.* The left- or right-hand man of the leading file will halt and the remainder will halt and dress as they reach their places.

iii. The squad may be formed obliquely to the line of march by the command *Half (or quarter) Left (or right) Form—Squad.*

4. Forming single file and two deep.

Advance in Single File from the Right. Quick—March.

The front rank man of the right file will march off, followed by his rear rank man, who will be followed by the front rank man of the second file, and so on.

Notes.—i. If the squad is halted in file, the command will be *Advance in Single File, Quick—March.* If the squad is marching in file the command will be *Form—Single File.* The front rank man of the leading file will then lead on, the remainder marking time to get into their places, and following on as described above.

ii. A squad may similarly advance in single file from fours.

Form—Two-deep.

The leading man will mark time, the remainder of the squad will regain their positions in file, marking time as they reach their places.

(B 10984)   C

Forward.

The squad will move forward in file.

Note.—If it is desired to halt on completion of the movement, the command will be *At the Halt Form Two—Deep,* when the leading man will halt, the remainder halting as they reach their places in file.

42. *The formation of fours and elementary training in march discipline.*

1. Column of fours is the ordinary marching formation of infantry on a road, and is then known as column of route. The greatest attention should be paid to training the recruit to keep the prescribed distance from, and to cover exactly, the man in front. Order, comfort, and the reduction of fatigue depend on the maintenance of exact distance by each four. Exact covering and dressing when moving in fours is to be kept even when marching at ease, unless orders to the contrary are issued.

Odd numbers are right files, and even numbers left files.

2. In order that the left four may always be complete, the file on the left of a squad will always act as a left file, and the second file from the left as a right file in forming fours.

3. A test of good marching in fours is the position of the men when they turn into line. If there are no gaps or irregularities in the line, and the squad occupies the same frontage as before it formed fours, the marching is good. This test should be frequently applied during the instruction of recruits, and the slightest carelessness as regards the maintenance of the exact distance should be checked at once.

PLATE IV.   *To face p. 43.*

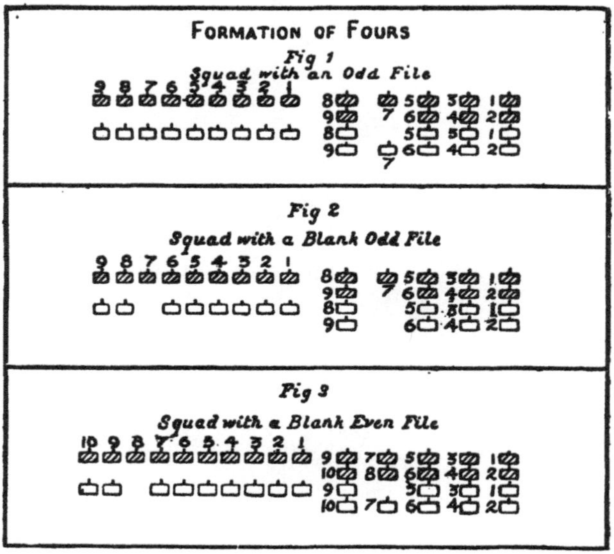

FORMATION OF FOURS

Fig 1
Squad with an Odd File

Fig 2
Squad with a Blank Odd File

Fig 3
Squad with a Blank Even File

4. Units moving in fours will march on the extreme left of roads. The left will always direct and, during halts, men will fall out on the left of the road. It is of great importance when large forces are moving that a portion of the road is kept absolutely clear of troops for the passage of traffic and communication of orders, and it is necessary that the soldier should be accustomed from the first to marching in this manner, *e.g.*, when marching to and from the range, when fatigue parties are marching to and from their work, &c.

43. *Forming fours* (Plate IV).

1. *In line in two ranks at the halt.*

Form—Fours.

The left files will take a pace of 30 inches back with the left foot, and then a side pace of 27 inches with the right, so as to cover their right files. In this formation the squad will stand in fours.

Form—Two-deep.

The left files will move to their original position in line by taking a side pace of 27 inches with the left foot and a pace forward of 30 inches with the right ; or if the squad has been turned about while in fours, a side pace with the right foot and a pace back with the left.

Note.—In forming fours after changing ranks, left files will take a pace of 30 inches to their front with the right foot, and one of 27 inches to the left with the left, thus bringing them into the same relative position as regards right files as they occupy after forming fours in the usual way.

They will form two-deep by taking a side pace with the right foot and a pace back with the left.

2. *To the right or left.*

Form—Fours.

As above.

Right.

Each man of the squad will turn in the named direction.

Note.—Except during the elementary training of recruits, the command *Form—Fours, Right (or Left)* will, in cases where no other caution is indicated in this manual, be preceded by the caution *Move to the Right (or left) in Fours,* whether troops are halted or on the march.

3. *To re-form line.*

Left (*or* Right)—Turn.

Each man of the squad will turn in the direction named, and then form two-deep, as described above.

Note.—If it is required to remain in fours, the word of command will be *In Fours, Left (or right)—Turn.*

4. *When on the march in line.*

Form—Fours, Right.

As in 2 and 3, but the right files will mark time two paces, while the left files are moving to their places.

Note.—Should the command *Right (or left)—Incline* be given instead of *Right (or left)* the squad will incline instead of turning in the required direction.

When inclining the squad will remain in fours.

5. *When in file, at the halt or on the march.*

Form—Fours.

The left files will move forward into their position in fours if a right file is leading, or back if a left file is leading.

If on the move, the right files will mark time two paces.

Form—Two-deep.

The left files will move up or fall back into their places in file. If on the move, the right files will mark time two paces.

Note.—When a squad is moving in fours it will always march and dress by the left.

44. *Movements in fours.*

1. *Changing direction.*

Right (*or* Left)—Wheel.

The inner man of the leading four will move round a quarter of the circumference of a circle having a radius of 4 feet, stepping short to enable the other men of the four to wheel with him. When the quarter circle is completed the four leads on in the new direction. The other fours in succession will follow in the footsteps of the leading four without increasing or diminishing their distances from each other or altering the time.

2. Rear Fours—Cover.

If the squad is halted or ordered to mark time before the whole squad has wheeled into the new direction, the fours which have not yet wheeled will cover off on those which have, moving to their places by the shortest route.

3. *Forming squad when moving to a flank.*

On the Left (*or* Right), Form—Squad.

The squad will first form two deep, and will then act as a squad marching in file (*see* Sec. **41**, 3).

Forward.

The squad will move on in line in the direction in which it was originally marching in fours.

See notes to Sec. **41**, 3, which apply equally.

45. *The passage of obstacles.*

1. When a stream, ditch, bank, or similar obstacle is to be crossed it will generally be found better to increase rather than diminish the front by causing the men to open out gradually before they arrive at the obstacle.

2. It is frequently advisable to point out a place on the far side of the obstacle, and order the men to form up in a named formation at that place ; each man will then find his own way across.

3. If a line is to pass a narrow place, its front may be reduced by forming fours, file, or single file to a flank or inwards ; or fours may be formed and closed to a flank or on the centre.

4. If a narrow place has to be passed through in column it is important to avoid checks. It is therefore advisable to increase the pace during the passage, if it is not so long as to cause undue fatigue to the men.

46. *Dismissing with or without arms.*

Squad—Dismiss.

The squad will turn to the right, and, after a pause, break off quietly and leave the parade ground.

Notes.—i. If the squad is under arms, arms will be sloped before the squad is dismissed (except in Rifle regiments). But on wet days, to avoid damaging the uniform with wet rifles, troops may be dismissed at the order.

ii. If an officer is on parade the men will salute together before they break off.

2. SQUAD DRILL WITH ARMS.

RIFLE EXERCISES.

47. General rules.

1. Recruits, before they commence the rifle exercises, are to be taught the names of the different parts of the rifle and the care of arms.

2. The rifle exercises will not be performed at inspections, and will only be practised by units larger than a squad for purposes of ceremonial.

3. Instruction in the rifle exercises should be combined with aiming and firing instruction.

Squad drill with arms should be practised occasionally in extended order (*see* Chap. **V**) to accustom recruits to handle their arms steadily and correctly when separated from their comrades.

4. The following instructions apply to the short Lee-Enfield, Lee-Enfield, and Lee-Metford rifle. A special note is made when the instructions for the short Lee-Enfield rifle do not apply to the Lee-Enfield or Lee-Metford rifle.

5. The recruit having been thoroughly instructed in the rifle exercises by numbers, will be taught to perform them in quick time, the words of command being given without the numbers, and executed as detailed in the following sections, with a pause of one beat of quick time between each motion.

6. Squads drilling with rifles will be practised in the different marches and variations of step described in the foregoing sections.

The disengaged arm will be allowed to swing naturally as described in Secs. **21** and **24**.

48. *Falling in with arms at the order* (Plate V).

The recruit will fall in as described in Sec. **27**, with the rifle held perpendicularly at his right side, the butt on the ground, its toe in line with the toe of the right foot. The right arm to be slightly bent, the hand to hold the rifle at or near the band (with the Lee-Enfield or Lee-Metford rifle, near the lower band), back of the hand to the right, thumb against the thigh, fingers together and slanting towards the ground.

When each man has got his dressing he will *stand at ease*.

49. *To stand at ease from the order.*

Stand at—Ease.

Keeping the legs straight, carry the left foot about 12 inches to the left so that the weight of the body rests equally on both feet. At the same time incline the muzzle of the rifle slightly to the front with the right hand, arm close to the side, the left arm to be kept in the position of *attention.*

Note.—The procedure is the same with or without bayonets fixed.

50. *The attention from stand at ease.*

Squad—Attention.

The left foot will be brought up to the right and the rifle returned to the *order.*

51. *The slope from the order.*

Slope Arms—One.

Give the rifle a cant upwards with the right hand, catching it with the left hand at the back-sight and the right hand

PLATE V. *To face p.* **48.**

PLATE VL.   *To face p.* 49.

at the small of the butt, thumb to the left, elbow to the rear.

Two. (Plate VI.)

Carry the rifle across the body, and place it flat on the left shoulder, magazine outwards from the body. Seize the butt with the left hand, the first two joints of the fingers grasping the upper side of the butt, the thumb about one inch above the toe, the upper part of the left arm close to the side, the lower part horizontal, and the heel of the butt in line with the centre of the left thigh.

Three.

Cut away the right hand to the side.

52. *The order from the slope.*

Order Arms—One.

Bring the rifle down to the full extent of the left arm, at the same time meeting it with the right hand between the back sight and the band (at the lower band, Lee-Enfield and Lee-Metford rifle), arm close to the body.

Two.

Bring the rifle to the right side, seizing it at the same time with the left hand round the nose cap (at the upper band, Lee-Enfield and Lee-Metford rifle), butt just clear of the ground.

Three.

Place the butt quietly on the ground, cutting the left hand away to the side.

53. *The present from the slope.*

Present Arms—One.

Seize the rifle with the right hand at the small, both arms close to the body.

Two.

Raise the rifle with the right hand perpendicularly in front of the centre of the body, sling to the left ; at the same time place the left hand smartly on the stock, wrist on the magazine, fingers pointing upwards, thumb close to the forefinger, point of the thumb in line with the mouth ; the left elbow to be close to the butt, the right elbow and butt close to the body.

Three.   (Plate VII.)

Bring the rifle down perpendicularly close in front of the centre of the body, guard to the front, holding it lightly at the full extent of the right arm, fingers slanting downwards, and meet it smartly with the left hand immediately behind the back-sight, thumb pointing towards the muzzle ; at the same time place the hollow of the right foot against the left heel, both knees straight.   The weight of the rifle to be supported by the left hand.

54. *The slope from the present.*

Slope Arms—One.

Bring the right foot in line with the left and place the rifle on the left shoulder as described in the second motion of the *slope* from the *order*.

Two.

Cut away the right hand to the side.

PLATE VII. *To face p.* 50.

55. *The present from the order (for Rifle regiments only).*

Present Arms—One.

Give the rifle a cant upwards with the right hand, catching it with the left hand behind the back-sight, and the right hand at the small of the butt, thumb to the left, elbow to the rear.

Two.

Bring the rifle to a perpendicular position in front of the centre of the body, turning the sling to the left ; at the same time place the left hand smartly on the stock, wrist on the magazine, fingers pointing upwards, thumb close to the forefinger, point of the thumb in line with the mouth ; left elbow close to the butt, right elbow and butt close to the body.

Three.

As in the third motion of the *present* from the *slope.*

56. *The order from the present (for Rifle regiments only).*

Order Arms—One.

Carry the rifle to the right side and seize it with the right hand at the band (with Lee-Enfield or Lee-Metford rifle, at the lower band), and with the left hand close below the nose-cap (with Lee-Enfield or Lee-Metford rifle, below the upper band), butt just clear of the ground ; at the same time bring the right foot smartly up to the left.

Two.

Place the butt quietly on the ground as at the *order*, cutting the left hand away to the side.

57. *To fix bayonets from the order.*

Fix Bayonets—One.

Seize the handle of the bayonet with the left hand, knuckles to the front, thumb and fingers to the rear; at the same time push the muzzle of the rifle sharply forward and turn the head and eyes to the right, the right-hand man looking to the left.

Two. (Plate VIII.)

Taking the time from the right-hand man, draw the bayonet, turning the point upwards and keeping the elbow down. Place the handle on the bayonet standard, with the ring over the stud on the nose-cap (with the Lee-Enfield or Lee-Metford rifle, over the muzzle), pressing it home to the catch. Body and head to be erect.

Three.

Taking the time from the right-hand man (who will raise his disengaged arm to the full extent and in line with the shoulder), bring the rifle to the *order;* at the same time cut away the left hand to the side, turning the head and eyes to the front.

Note.—On the word *Fix*, the right-hand man of the unit will take three paces forward, resuming his place in line when the third motion is completed.

58. *Unfixing bayonets.*

Unfix Bayonets—One. (Plate IX.)

Keeping the heels closed, place the rifle between the knees, guard to the front, and grasp the handle of the bayonet with the right hand, knuckles to the front, thumb of left hand

PLATE VIII.   *To face p. 52.*

PLATE IX.

To face p. 53.

on bayonet bolt spring; draw the rifle into the body with
the knees, and press the spring. Raise the bayonet about
1 inch, and at the same time turn the head and eyes to the
left.

Two.

Taking the time from the left-hand man, raise the bayonet
off the bayonet standard, drop the point to the left side,
ring to the rear, and, raising the right hand, seize the scabbard with the left hand and guide the bayonet into it.

Three.

Taking the time from the left-hand man (who will look
inwards and raise his right arm), force the bayonet home,
and bring the right hand to the band (Lee-Enfield and Lee-
Metford rifle, to the lower band).

Four.

Taking the time from the left-hand man, cut away the
left hand to the side and return to the *order*, turning the head
and eyes to the front.

Note.—On the word *Unfix*, the left-hand man of the unit
will take three paces forward, resuming his place in line
when the fourth motion is completed.

59. *Inspection of arms.*

1. For Inspection, Port—Arms.

Cant the rifle, muzzle leading, with the right hand smartly
across the body, guard to the left and downwards, the barrel
crossing opposite the point of the left shoulder, and meet
it at the same time with the left hand close behind the back-
sight, thumb and fingers round the rifle, the left wrist to be
opposite the left breast, both elbows close to the body.

Turn the safety catch completely over to the front with the thumb or forefinger of the right hand (with Lee-Enfield or Lee-Metford rifle, lower the safety catch with the thumb of the right hand). Pull out the cut-off if closed, first pressing it downwards with the thumb, then seize the knob with the forefinger and thumb of the right hand, turn it sharply upwards, and draw back the bolt to its full extent, then grasp the butt with the right hand immediately behind the bolt, thumb pointing to the muzzle.

Note.—A squad, before being inspected, will receive the command *Rear Rank, One Pace Step Back—March.*

2. *To ease springs and come to the order.*

Ease—Springs.

From the position described above, work the bolt rapidly backwards and forwards until all cartridges are removed from the magazine and chamber* allowing them to fall to the ground, then close the breech (with Lee-Enfield or Lee-Metford rifle, the cut off should first be closed), press the trigger, close the cut off by placing the right hand over the bolt and pressing the cut off inwards, turn the safety catch over to the rear, and return the hand to the small.

Or, if the magazine is charged.

Lock—Bolt.

Close the breech (with Lee-Enfield or Lee-Metford rifle, the cut off should first be closed), then turn the safety catch over to the rear (with Lee-Enfield or Lee-Metford rifle raise the safety catch) and return the hand to the small.

---

* This precaution will also be adopted when magazines are not charged.

Order Arms—One.

Holding the rifle firmly in the left hand, seize it with the right hand at the band (with Lee-Enfield or Lee-Metford rifle, at the lower band).

Two.

As in the second motion of the *order* from the *slope.*

Three.

As in the third motion of the *order* from the *slope.*

60. *Instructions for inspecting arms.*

1. When arms are inspected at the *port* only, as in inspecting a platoon on parade, the officer or non-commissioned officer will see that the exterior of the rifle is clean and free from rust ; that the magazine and action are clean and in good order ; that the sights are at zero ; and that no parts are loose or damaged. He will here and there examine the bore of a rifle to see that it has been cleaned and oiled and is free from obstructions.

2. Each soldier, when the officer has passed the file next to him, will, without further word of command, *ease springs, order arms,* and *stand at ease.*

When the inspection is completed, the squad will be closed on the squad commander's command *Close Ranks—March,* when the rear rank will take one pace forward.

61. *To examine arms.*

Examine—Arms.

Both ranks, being at the *port*, will come to the position for loading (*see* Musketry Regulations, Part I, para. 242), with the muzzle so inclined as to enable the officer to look through the barrel, the thumb-nail of the right hand being placed in front of the bolt to reflect light into the barrel.

The soldier, when the officer has passed the next file to him, will act as detailed in Sec. **60**, 2.

Notes.—i. If it is necessary to examine arms, the men, when in the position of *for inspection, port arms,* will be cautioned to remain at the *port.* Ranks will be closed, as in Sec. **60**, 2, when the examination has been completed.

ii. In ordering arms from the examine, the first motion is to seize the rifle with the right hand between the back-sight and the band, at the same time bringing the left foot back to the right. With the second motion the rifle will be brought to the order, the left hand being cut away to the side.

62. *To trail arms from the order, and vice versâ* (Plate X).

1. Trail—Arms.

By a slight bend of the right arm give the rifle a cant forward and seize it at the point of balance, bringing it at once to a horizontal position at the side at the full extent of the right arm, which should hang easily from the shoulder, fingers and thumb round the rifle.

2. Order—Arms.

Raise the muzzle, catch the rifle at the band (with Lee-Enfield or Lee-Metford rifle at the lower band) and come to the *order.*

Note.—The *trail* is not to be used in close order drill except by rifle regiments.

It will be used when required for movements in the field in both close and extended order.

PLATE X.   *To face p. 56.*

63. *The shoulder from the order, and vice versâ (for Rifle regiments only).*

1. Shoulder Arms—One.

Give the rifle a cant upwards with the right hand, catching it with the left hand in line with the elbow; at the same time, slipping the second finger of the right hand inside the guard, close the first and second fingers on the magazine, thumb and remaining fingers pointing downwards; the upper part of the barrel to rest in the hollow of the shoulder.

Two.

Drop the left hand to the side.

2. Order Arms—One.

Relax the grasp of the right hand and allow the rifle to drop till the butt is within two inches of the ground.   At the same time seize the rifle with the left hand at the nose cap and with the right hand at the band.

Two.

Place the butt quietly on the ground as at the *order*, cutting the left hand to the side.

64. *The shoulder from the trail, and vice versâ (for Rifle regiments only).*

1. Shoulder Arms—One.

Tightening the grasp of the right hand, bring the rifle to a perpendicular position, and hold it with the left hand in line with the elbow, then seize it with the right hand at the *shoulder*.

Two.

Drop the left hand to the side.

2. Trail Arms—One.

Seize the rifle with the left hand in line with the elbow, arm close to the body.

Two.

Grasp the rifle with the right hand at the point of balance ; then bring it down to the *trail*, at the same time dropping the left hand to the side.

Note.—Rifle regiments march at the *shoulder* when moving in file, the men shouldering their arms on the command *Quick—March*, or, if already on the move, on the command which brings them into file.

65. *The short trail.*

No word of command.

Raise the rifle about 3 inches from the ground, keeping it otherwise in the position of the *order*.

If standing with ordered arms, and directed to form fours, to close to the right or left, to step back, or to take any named number of paces forward, men will come to the *short trail*.

66. *Fixing bayonets on the march.*

Fix—Bayonets.

1. When at the *slope* seize the rifle with the right hand at the point of balance and bring it to the *trail*, with the muzzle sloping upwards in front of the right breast. Draw and fix the bayonet with the left hand. Bring the rifle to the *slope*.

2. When at the *trail* raise the muzzle of the rifle and proceed as above described.

67. *To change arms when at the slope.*

Change Arms—One.

Seize the butt of the rifle with the right hand, back of the hand up, at the same time slipping the left hand up to the small.

Two.

Carry the rifle, turning the magazine outwards, on to the right shoulder, bringing it well to the front, so as to clear the head.

Three.

Cut the left hand to the side.

Note.—To change arms from the right to the left shoulder act as above, reading left for right, and right for left.

68. *To change arms from the trail.*

Change Arms—One.

Bring the rifle to a perpendicular position in front of the right shoulder, magazine to the front, upper part of the arm close to the side, forearm horizontal, hand in line with the waistbelt.

Two.

Pass the rifle across the front of the body, catching it with the left hand at the point of balance, at the same time cutting the right hand smartly to the side. In this position the rifle is to be held perpendicular and opposite the left shoulder, magazine to the front, upper part of the left arm close to the side, left forearm horizontal, hand in line with the waist-belt.

Three.

Lower the rifle to the full extent of the left arm at the *trail.*

(B 10984)   **D**

69. *To sling arms from the order.*

Sling—Arms.

The sling of the rifle having been loosened to the full extent, the soldier will pass his head and right arm between the sling and rifle, muzzle upwards, rifle hanging diagonally across the back.

Note.—The rifle is carried slung by dismounted signallers, and drivers leading pack animals.

70. *To ground arms and take up arms, from and to the order.*

Ground—Arms.

Place the rifle gently on the ground at the right side, magazine to the right, muzzle pointing in the same direction as the right foot. The right hand will be in line with the toe as it places the rifle on the ground. Then return smartly to the position of *attention*.

Take up—Arms.

Bend down, take up the rifle, and return to the *order*.

71. *Piling arms.*

Pile Arms—One.

The squad being in two ranks at the *order*, the rear rank will take a pace forward and turn the barrels of their rifles towards the front rank. The front rank will turn about and place the butts of their rifles between their feet.

Two.

The odd numbers of the front rank will incline the muzzles towards those of the even numbers, barrels downwards, slipping the right hand to the nose cap; the odd numbers will then seize the rifles of the even numbers with the left hand in the same manner and hold up the piling swivels of both rifles with the forefingers and thumbs, crossing the muzzles to bring the swivels together.   The even numbers will drop the right hand to the side.

Three.

The even numbers of the rear rank, holding their rifles sling upwards at the band (Lee-Enfield and Lee-Metford rifles at the lower band), will incline the muzzles forward, and with the left hand will link swivels through the crossed muzzles of the front rank, raising their butts as high as necessary to do so.   The odd numbers of the front rank will now turn the barrels of their rifles towards the even numbers of the rear rank, who will then place the heels of their butts 6 inches to the right of the toe of the right foot so as to make the pile secure.

Four.

The odd numbers of the rear rank will lodge their rifles against the pile, and will then drop their hands to the side.

Stand—Clear.

Ranks will step back one pace and turn to the right flank.

72. *Unpiling arms.*

Stand—To.

Ranks will turn inwards and take a pace forward.

Unpile Arms—One.

The whole will seize their rifles at the band (Lee-Enfield and Lee-Metford rifles, at the lower band).

(B 10984)   D 2

Two.

Swivels will be unlinked, by raising and inclining the butts inwards, and rifles brought to the *order*.

Three.

The left-hand man of the front rank will raise his disengaged arm. When he sees that the whole are ready he will drop his arm, when the front rank will turn about and the rear rank will step back a pace.

Note.—In piling arms on parade, the command *Fall—Out* will be given after *Stand—Clear*. On again falling in, the men will place themselves as they stood before falling out.

73. *Paying compliments with arms.*

1. When a soldier, other than a rifleman, carrying a rifle, passes or addresses an officer he will do so at the *slope*, and will salute by carrying the right hand smartly to the small of the butt, forearm horizontal, back of the hand to the front, fingers straight (Plate XI). He will salute on the third pace before reaching him, and will cut the hand away on the third pace after passing him.

2. A rifleman when passing an officer will do so at the *shoulder*; when addressing an officer he will do so at the *order*.

3. In passing an officer the soldier will always turn his head towards him in the same manner as when unarmed.

4. A soldier, if halted when an officer passes, will turn towards him and stand at the *order*.

74. *Guards and sentries.*

1. Guards, including reliefs, rounds, and patrols, will

PLATE XI.   *To face p.* 62.

march with sloped arms and bayonets fixed ; those belonging
to Rifle regiments with trailed arms.

2. Sentries are to walk with their arms at the *slope*, except
those of Rifle regiments, who will carry their arms at the
trail.

Sentries, except those of Rifle regiments, when saluting
will halt, turn to the front, and, except when presenting
arms, carry the right hand to the small of the butt as
directed above.   Sentries of Rifle regiments will, in similar
circumstances, halt, front, and *shoulder*.

3. Further instructions concerning guards and sentries
are given in King's Regulations and in " Ceremonial."

CHAPTER III.

SECTION AND PLATOON DRILL.

75. *Section drill.*

The section will be exercised in all the movements of squad drill, the word *section* being substituted for *squad*.

PLATOON DRILL.

76. *Object of platoon drill.*

1. The object of platoon drill is to enable the platoon, when it takes its place in the company, to carry out both by day and night any movement or formation the company commander may direct, whether laid down in this manual or improvised to meet the circumstances of the moment.

77. *General rules.*

1. The platoon may be formed as follows :—

    i.   In line (as in squad drill).
    ii. In column of fours, or in file (as in squad drill).
    iii. In line of sections in fours or file (*see* Secs. **79-80**).

2. The platoon commander and platoon serjeant, when the platoon is acting alone or at a distance from other platoons, will place themselves where they can best exercise supervision. The normal position of commanders and supernumeraries is shown on Plates XII and XIV.

3. Plate XIV refers to column of route only. In all other movements in fours, except as noted in Secs. **79, 80, 86, 4,** and **87, 5,** commanders and supernumeraries retain the relative positions they occupied before fours were formed.

4. The left will be named as the directing flank when

PLATE XII.   *To face p.* **64.**

POSITIONS OF COMMANDERS, ETC., IN A PLATOON.

A platoon in line.

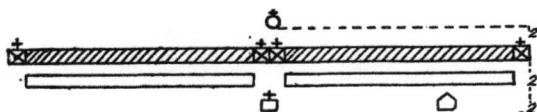

— Key —

Ŏ = *Platoon Comdr.*

⊡ = *Platoon Serjt.*

⊠ = *Section Comdr.*

⌂ = *Drummer.*

increasing frontage on the right, or when the left is the pivot flank.

The left will always direct in column of route.

With the above exceptions the right will always direct unless otherwise ordered.

5. *Guides.*—When a platoon is in line the section commander on the directing flank acts as guide and is responsible for the maintenance of direction.   In column of fours or in file this responsibility devolves upon the man on the directing flank of the leading four or leading file.   In line of sections in fours or file, the leading man on the inner flank of the directing section will be responsible for direction, and the leading man on the inner flank of each of the other units for the correct interval.

6. Supernumeraries will conform to all orders given to the platoon as regards the carrying of their arms.

7. Before a movement in close order is made, arms will be sloped.   In Rifle regiments, which drill in close order at the trail, the men will trail arms on the command *Quick* or *Double March*, and will halt and stand at ease on the command or signal *Halt*.

8. Units will frequently be practised in reassembling when dispersed.

9. When an officer requires to pass through the ranks the two files immediately opposite to him will make way on the command *Make Way* by taking a pace to the rear and a side pace outwards, so as to cover the files on their flanks.   They will resume their position as soon as the officer has passed through.

10. When a unit in close order is on the move and is required to halt as soon as a change of formation has been completed, the command will be preceded by the caution *At the Halt*.

78. *Inspecting and telling off a platoon.*

Unless otherwise ordered, the platoon will fall in for inspection by its commander in line. The inspection will usually be carried out as follows :—

Platoon—Attention. Fix—Bayonets.
Rear Rank, One Pace Step Back—March.

The appointments, clothing, etc., will then be inspected.

Unfix Bayonets, For Inspection, Port—Arms.
Examine Arms (if required).

Arms will then be inspected as in Secs. **59-61.**

Platoon—Attention. Close Ranks—March.
By Sections—Number. Form—Fours. Form—Two Deep.

To avoid unnecessary loss of road space in column of route it is advisable, when sections are weak, that two or more sections should be numbered off and proved together for the purpose of forming fours. This numbering must not preclude sections from being separated under their own leaders for movements in line of sections in file or single file, or for any individual action required.

79. *A platoon in line forming a line of sections in fours or file moving in the same direction.*

Advance in Fours (or File) from the Right of Sections. Form—Fours, Right (or Right—Turn). Sections, Left—Wheel, Quick—March.

The platoon will move as directed, section commanders placing themselves two paces in front of the leading four or file of their respective sections.

Notes.—i. In order to re-form line the command will be *On the Left, Form Sections,* on which the men will act as in squad drill.   Formation will be made on the leading guides.

ii. If on the march, the words *Quick March* are omitted.

iii. When a line of sections in fours or file is on the march the interval may be increased or diminished on the command *From* (or *On*) *No.   , Open* (or *Close*) *to* — *Paces Interval, Remainder, Double—March.*

80.   *A platoon in column of fours forming a line of sections in fours or file, moving in the same direction.*

On the left, Form Line of Sections in Fours (or File), at — Paces Interval ; Remainder, Double—March.

If file has been ordered, the whole will first form two deep.   The leading section will then move forward in quick time, and the remainder will be led by the shortest route to the positions at the named interval, where their commanders will give *Quick—March,* taking post two paces in front of their leading four or file.

Note.—i. This movement can also be performed at the halt.

ii. The movements in Secs. **79** and **80** can also be carried out in single file.

CHAPTER IV.

COMPANY DRILL.

81. *Object of company drill.*

The object of company drill is to train the four platoons to work together as parts of the same tactical unit, and to acquire flexibility and the power of rapid manœuvre within the company.

82. *General rules.*

1. The company may be formed as follows :—

    (i) In line.
    (ii) In close column of platoons.
    (iii) In column of platoons.
    (iv) In column of fours or in file.
    (v) In line of platoons or sections in fours or file.

2. The positions of all commanders and supernumeraries in the various formations are shown in Plates XIII and XIV, but during drill and manœuvre the company commander and second in command will place themselves where they can best exercise supervision.

The positions of the company second in command, the company serjeant-major, and the company quarter-master-serjeant, as shown in Plate XIII, remain the same, whether the company is by the right or by the left.

3. *Guides.*—In line, and in column of platoons, the section commander, or commanders, on the directing flank, will act as guide or guides and be responsible for the maintenance of direction and distance. In lines of platoons or sections in fours or file the leading man on the inner flank of the directing

PLATE XIII.   *To face p. 68.*

POSITIONS OF COMMANDERS, ETC., IN A COMPANY.

FIG. 1.

A company in line.

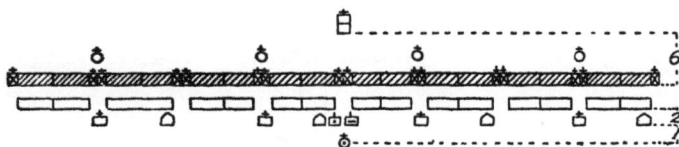

FIG. 2.

*A company in
column of platoons.*

Note.—In line, column,
or close column of
platoons, platoon
commanders are
two paces in front
of the centre of
their commands.

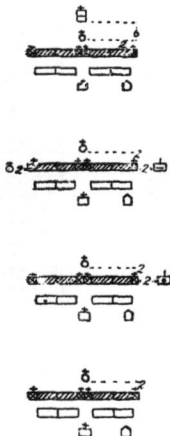

— Key —

= Company Comdr.

= *do·* Second in Comd.

= Platoon Comdr.

= Company Serj + Maj.

= *-do-* Q.M.Serj +.

= Platoon Serj +

= Section Comdr.

= Drummer.

PLATE XIV.　　　To face p. 69.

POSITIONS OF COMMANDERS, ETC., IN A COMPANY IN
COLUMN OF ROUTE.

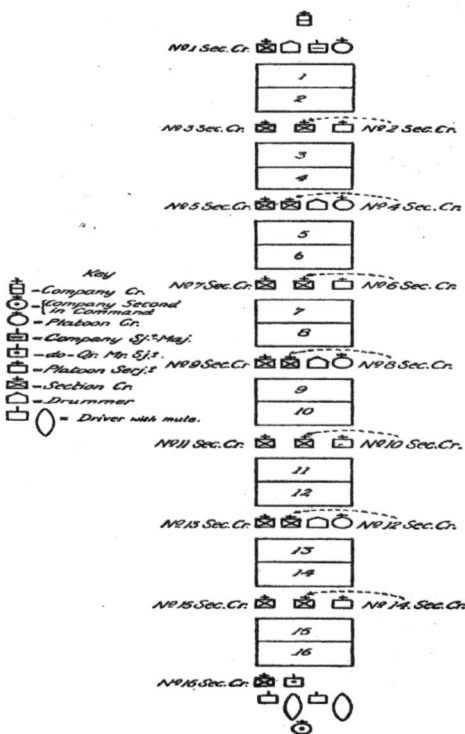

No.1 Sec. Cr.

1	
2	

No.3 Sec. Cr.　　　　No.2 Sec. Cr.

3	
4	

No.5 Sec. Cr.　　　　No.4 Sec. Cr.

5	
6	

Key

☐ = Company Cr.
☉ = Company Second in Command
○ = Platoon Cr.
☐ = Company Sj:-Maj:
☐ = do - Qr: Mr: Sj.s
☐ = Platoon Serj:t
☒ = Section Cr.
○ = Drummer
☐○ = Driver with mule.

No.7 Sec. Cr.　　　　No.6 Sec. Cr.

7	
8	

No.9 Sec. Cr.　　　　No.8 Sec. Cr.

9	
10	

No.11 Sec. Cr.　　　　No.10 Sec. Cr.

11	
12	

No.13 Sec. Cr.　　　　No.12 Sec. Cr.

13	
14	

No.15 Sec. Cr.　　　　No.14 Sec. Cr.

15	
16	

No.16 Sec. Cr.

unit will be responsible for direction ; the leading man on the inner flank of each of the other units for maintaining the correct interval.

4. In action or in high wind it will often be impossible for words of command to be heard. The company commander should therefore frequently practise his command in working by signal (*see* Sec. **94**).

5. The general rules for platoon drill enumerated in Sec. **77**, paras. 3-10, apply equally to company drill.

6. Unless otherwise ordered, a company will fall in for inspection in column of platoons, and will be inspected and proved as in Sec. **78**.

Notes.—i. In the following detail the title of the drill movement is shown in *italics*, and is followed by the company commander's caution or word of command in **thick type**. The detail of the movement then follows, in which orders to be given by platoon commanders are printed in *italics*. The company commander's cautions or words of command, when referred to in the detail, are printed in SMALL CAPITALS.

ii. When cautions and commands are given for formations to or from one flank only, the same rule applies when forming to or from the other flank.

iii. Movements and formations for which detail is given in fours can also be made in file or single file.

83. *A company changing ranks when halted.*

About—Turn.

The whole will turn about except officers and supernumeraries, who will regain their positions by passing round the flanks or through the ranks of the company, section commanders making way for them on the command *Make way,* by placing themselves between the files on their right or left, and afterwards aligning themselves with the front rank.

Note.—If ranks are changed on the march, section commanders will make way by checking the pace slightly and inclining outwards.

84. *Close column movements.*

1. *A close column changing direction.*

Change Direction Right, Right—Wheel.

The company, except the leading platoon, will make a partial turn to the left ; the leading platoon will not turn, but will look to the right.

Each man will move round on the circumference of a circle of which the right of the leading platoon is the centre.   The outer flank will direct, but when platoons are of unequal strength they will maintain the same relative positions as they held before the wheel.   The second in command will superintend the wheel on the left flank, the company serjeant-major on the right, and the former must, in regulating the pace, watch the left guide of the rear platoon, who will continue to march at a full pace throughout, and on whose movement the march of every man in the company should be made to depend.

When the company has circled round to the required angle, the command FORWARD, MARK TIME, or HALT will be given, on which all will at once turn in the required direction.

Notes.—i. When wheeling to the left, it will be the duty of the company serjeant-major to watch the right guide of the rear platoon as above.

ii. A close column moving in fours will wheel as above,

the leading four of each platoon wheeling in the same manner
as the leading platoon above, the fours in rear making a
partial turn outwards and following round after the leading
fours.

2. *A close column forming column of fours.*

**Advance (or Retire) in Fours from the Right.　Form
　　Fours—Right.**

The commander of the leading (or rear) platoon will give :
Left (or *Right*) *wheel, Quick—March*, and each platoon commander will act similarly in time to gain his place in column
of fours.

3. *A close column forming line facing in the same direction.*

(i) **On the Left, Form—Line.　　Remainder, Left—Turn,
　　Quick—March.**

The leading platoon will stand fast.　The remainder will
be led by their guides by the shortest route to the spot where
their inner flank will rest.　Each platoon will then wheel
parallel to the alignment and when opposite to its place in
line will be halted and turned to the right by its commander.

Note.—When companies are strong, the command—
REMAINDER, FORM—FOURS, LEFT, will be given instead of
REMAINDER, LEFT—TURN.

(ii) **Line—Outwards, One (*or* Two) Platoons to the
　　Right.　Remainder, Form—Fours, Outwards,
　　Quick—March.**

The movement will be made on the above principle.　The
platoon or platoons next in succession from the front will
move to the named flank.

When line has been formed the company commander will name a flank of direction.

4. *A close column on the march forming line facing a flank.*

At the Halt, Facing Left, Form—Line.

The commander of the rear platoon will at once give *At the Halt, Left—Form.* Each of the other commanders will form his platoon into line in like manner when it arrives at column distance from the platoon next in rear.

5. *Advancing in column from c'ose column.*

Advance in—Column.

The commander of the leading platoon will give *By the Right, Quick—March,* and the remaining platoons will be similarly marched off when the platoon next in front has reached column distance.

6. *A column on the march closing to close column.*

At the Halt, Form Close—Column (*or* Close Column at— Paces).

The leading platoon will at once be halted by its commander. * The remainder will be halted successively on reaching their positions in close column.

Note.—If it is required to continue moving after closing, the command will be FORM CLOSE COLUMN. REMAINDER, DOUBLE—MARCH, on which the leading platoon will continue to advance in quick time, the remainder taking up the quick time as they gain the correct distance.

85. *Column movements.*

1. *A column on the march changing direction.*

Change Direction—Right.

The commander of the leading platoon will give the command *Right—Form,* and, when the platoon is formed in the new direction, *Forward.* The remaining platoons, on arriving at the same point, will be formed successively in a similar manner.

Notes.—i. Before changing direction *left* a column should normally be ordered to march by the left.

ii. A column can similarly change direction half (or quarter) right.

2. *A column forming column of fours.*

Advance (*or* Retire) in Fours from the Right. Form Fours—Right. Platoons Left (*or* Right) Wheel, Quick—March.

Each platoon will move in the required direction, forming column of fours.

Note.—When a column is on the march, platoons may, if desired, advance in fours in succession. On the caution In succession advance in fours from the right the commander of the leading platoon will form fours right and wheel to the left. On arriving at the same point the commander of each succeeding platoon will act in a similar manner.

3. *A column forming line facing in the same direction.*

On the Left, Form—Line, Remainder Left—Incline, Quick—March.

The leading platoon will stand fast. The remainder will act as in squad drill. When each platoon is immediately in rear of its position in line, it will receive from its commander *Right—Incline*, and when on the alignment *Halt*.

Notes.—i. If the column is marching, the command DOUBLE MARCH instead of QUICK MARCH will be given, and on reaching the alignment *Quick March* instead of *Halt*.

ii. When companies are strong, the command FORM FOURS —LEFT instead of LEFT INCLINE will be given, and the movement will be carried out as described in Sec. **84**, para. 3 (i), Note.   Line may similarly be formed outwards, the words of command being as in Sec. **84**, para 3 (ii).   In both these cases the movement will be carried out at the halt.

4. *A column forming line facing a flank and moving forward.*

Into Line, Left—Form.   Quick—March.

The men will act as in squad drill, the left guide of each platoon acting, on the word FORM, as the pivot-man of a squad.

When line is formed the company commander will give FORWARD, BY THE LEFT.

86. *Line movements.*

1. *A line forming column (or close column) facing in the same direction.*

On the Right, Form Column (*or* Close Column) of Platoons.   Remainder, Right—Turn.   Quick—March.

The platoon on the right will stand fast.   The remainder will be led by their guides by the shortest route to their positions in column (or close column), where they will receive from their commanders *Halt, Left—Turn*.   On the word *Halt*, the right guides will at once turn to their left and

take up their covering and distance from the right guide of
the platoon in front.

Note.—When companies are strong, the command REMAIN-
DER FORM FOURS—RIGHT will be given instead of REMAINDER
RIGHT—TURN.

2. *A line advancing in column of platoons.*

**Advance in Column of Platoons from the Right.
Remainder, Right—Turn. Quick—March.**

The right platoon will advance. The remainder will act
as in squad drill, mark time two paces, and then lead on.
When the guide of each platoon is in rear of the centre of the
preceding platoon, the commander will give *Left—Incline*,
and on arriving in column of platoons, again *Left—Incline*.

Notes.—i. If on the march, the words QUICK MARCH are
omitted.

ii. When companies are strong the command REMAINDER
FORM FOURS—RIGHT will be given instead of REMAINDER,
RIGHT—TURN.

3. *A line forming column facing a flank.*

**At the Halt, into Column, Platoons, Right—Form.
Quick—March.**

The men will act as in squad drill, the right guide of each
platoon acting as the pivot man of a squad.

4. *A line forming a line of platoons in fours facing in the same
direction.*

**Advance in Fours from the Right of Platoons. Form
—Fours, Right. Platoons, Left—Wheel, Quick—
March.**

The movement will be made as directed, platoon com-

manders placing themselves two paces in front of the leading
four of their respective platoons; section commanders
maintaining the relative positions they occupied before fours
were formed.

Note.—A line of sections in fours or files can also be formed,
as in Sec. **79.**

87. *Movements from column of fours.*

1. *A column of fours forming forward into column of platoons.*

On the Left, Form—Platoons.

The men will act as in squad drill. Formation will be made
on the leading guide of each platoon. When column has been
formed the company commander will give FORWARD, BY THE
RIGHT.

Note.—A column of fours may, if desired, increase frontage
by platoons in succession, in which case the company commander will give the caution IN SUCCESSION, ON THE LEFT,
FORM—PLATOONS. The commander of the leading platoon
will at once give *On the Left, Form—Platoon* followed by
Forward, and on reaching the same point the remaining commanders will act in a similar manner.

2. *A column of fours forming forward into close column of platoons
    at the halt.*

**At the Halt, on the Left, Form Close Column of—
    Platoons.**

The commander of the leading platoon will at once give
At the Halt, On the Left, Form—Platoon. The commanders
of the remaining platoons on arriving at close column
distance will act in a similar manner.

3. *A column of fours forming column (or close column) of platoons at the halt facing a flank.*

At the Halt, Facing Left, Form Column (*or* Close Column) of—Platoons.

The commander of the leading platoon will halt his unit and turn it to the left.

The remainder will be led by their guides by the shortest route to their positions in column (or close column), where they will receive the command *Halt, Left—Turn.*

On the word *Halt,* the right guides will at once turn to their left and take up their covering and distance from the right guide of the platoon in front.

4. *A column of fours forming column facing a flank and moving forward.*

Facing Left, Advance in Column of—Platoons.

The commander of the leading platoon will give *Left— Turn.* The remainder will mark time two paces and then lead on in fours.

Each platoon commander, when the leading guide of his platoon is in rear of the centre of the preceding platoon, will give *Left incline,* and when in column, again *Left incline.*

5. *A column of fours forming a line of platoons in fours, moving in the same direction.*

On the Left, Form Line of Platoons in Fours at — Paces Interval.   Remainder, Double—March.

The leading platoon will continue to move forward in quick time. The remainder will be led by their guides by the shortest route to their positions in the alignment at the named interval, where platoon commanders will give the command *Quick—March,* taking post 2 paces in front of the leading four of their platoons.

Notes.—i. When companies are strong, it will be found more convenient to perform this movement at the halt, the advance being continued after the line of platoons has been formed.

ii. A line of sections in fours or file can similarly be formed, section commanders taking post two paces in front of their leading four or file.

88. *Movements in line, or lines, of small columns from any formation.*

1. These movements are of importance, as they form the link between close order drill and movements in battle. In carrying out such movements the principles laid down in Part II (Sec. **113**) are to be considered.

2. Constant practice is to be given in rapidly changing from any formation into a line or lines of platoons in fours or file, at varying intervals and distances.

From these formations lines of sections in file or single file on irregular frontages should be formed, the sections being subsequently extended as the requirements of the situation dictate.

3. The rapidity of such movements will depend on the clearness and completeness of the explanations and orders of the company commander.

4. In movements of this nature the number of executive words of command should be reduced to a minimum, and each unit should move to its place in the new formation by the shortest route and in the simplest manner, on the company

commander's order **Move** or prearranged signal. Units will subsequently be guided only by such methods of control as could be exercised in battle. (*See* Chapter V.)

89. *Dismissing.*

The officers will first be ordered to fall out, when they will move in quick time to the commander of the parade, salute, and await his orders.

The company will then be dismissed as in Sec. **46.**

CHAPTER V.

EXTENDED ORDER DRILL.

90. *The object of extended order drill.*

1. During his training in close order drill, the soldier will learn strict discipline and the habit of prompt and unquestioning obedience to orders; he should also be taught to march, to use his rifle, and to become a fair judge of distance.

Important as the above lessons are, however, it is, apart from the vital question of discipline, even more important that the soldier should learn the best methods of closing with an enemy, and concurrently with his other training he will be taught the elements of these methods by means of extended order drill.

2. It will be explained to the soldier that victory can rarely be won by fire alone, that the object of fire is to prepare the way for the charge with the bayonet, and that decisive success can only be gained by closing with the enemy.

3. In order to approach to within close range of a well-armed enemy by day it is usually necessary to advance with intervals between the men. This is called advancing in extended order. When close ranges are reached, the density of the front or firing line is increased until fire is developed from the greatest possible number of rifles on a given frontage.

4. The first stage, therefore, is for the soldier to learn to move in extended order formations. Other methods of advancing under fire are considered later. (*See* Part II.)

5. These formations are taught in two progressive stages :—

    (*a*) On the drill ground.

    (*b*) In the field, in conjunction with the uses of ground and fire. (*See* Sec. **108.**)

91. *Instructions for extended order drill.*

1. Extended order drill can be carried out by a company or any smaller unit. It will be begun during recruit training, and will be continued on a progressive system concurrently with section, platoon, and company drill in close order.

2. The tendency of open formations is to cause slovenly movement and inattention. If this fault should arise, it is advisable to revert from time to time to close order until it is eradicated.

3. In extended order there are several methods by which a leader can exercise control and maintain communication. In the field the occasions on which each should be adopted are determined by the requirements of the situation. In the drill stage of instruction it is sufficient to teach the soldier to work by each of the various methods, namely :—

    (i) Word of command. (*See* Sec. **93.**)

    (ii) Signal. (*See* Sec. **94.**)

    (iii) Whistle blasts and calls. (*See* Sec. **95.**)

    (iv) Verbal orders and messages passed from mouth to mouth. (*See* Sec. **96.**)

92. *General rules.*

1. The unit will first be formed in line, two deep, standing at ease.

2. On the move the rifle will be carried at the trail. In extending it will, if necessary, be carried at the short trail until there is sufficient room to trail.

3. It is important that men should always be trained with reference to an assumed position of the enemy. An objective will invariably be pointed out, towards which each man will turn when the unit is halted.

4. During preliminary training in extended order drill, the men, when halted, will always stand at ease without further word of command. When ordered to move, they will come to attention before they step off.

During a more advanced stage of instruction, when the hostile position is represented by a natural feature or dummy screens, the men will on halting lie down.

5. In action a large proportion of casualties usually occurs when men are getting up to advance, or when in the act of lying down. It is of great importance, therefore, that men should be taught to perform these movements in the quickest possible manner, and that, when ordered to advance, they should all rise instantly and move forward directly they have risen.

6. A new objective may be named as required. For instance, after changing direction a new objective would be required, unless it was intended again to change direction before halting.

7. Correct dressing and keeping step are not required, but an approximate line should be kept ; otherwise, when extended, men may mask one another's fire. A flank of direction will not be named as in close order drill, but at the beginning, or from time to time as required, a file of direction will be named to which the unit will look for the general alignment. When the unit is extended to single rank or to intervals, the front rank man of the named file will direct ; when closed two deep, that man of the named file who is in the leading rank.

8. Commanders should place themselves where they can best supervise their commands. Supernumeraries conform, and move in the positions relative to those which they occupied in line.

9. It should be explained that as extensions are usually
made in order to develop fire or to avoid loss, they are normally carried out at the double.   An extended line is closed
only when under cover or when not under fire ; closing is
therefore carried out in quick time unless it is desired to close
on the move.

10. Unless otherwise ordered men extend and close from or
to the centre file, which should be named.

11. The cautions before commencing drill are as follows :—

No. —   Centre File and File of Direction.   The
Objective is —.

The front rank man of the given file will prove by raising
the disengaged arm.   If it is required to march by a flank,
the front rank man of the file on that flank will prove.

93. *Control by word of command.*

1. *A unit in line extending from the halt to the halt.*

To—Paces, Extend.

The front rank man of the centre file will stand fast.   The
remainder will turn outwards and extend, or increase their
extensions, moving in double time.   The rear rank men
will form on the left of their front rank men.   Each man
is responsible that the given number of paces separate him
from the man who is next to him and nearer to the centre.

Notes.—i.   If it is required to extend to a flank, or from a
named file, the above command will be preceded by the
caution *To the right (or left), or from No.—.*

ii.   When extending on the move, the front rank man of
the file from which the extension is being made will continue
to advance in quick time, the remainder acting as above.

iii.   During a more advanced stage of instruction, rough and ready expedients for extending will be practised, in order to form a fighting front quickly in any direction from any formation. The men should be taught to act on such commands as *Line that bank, Extend along that hedge,* and so on.

2. *A unit marching in fours extending to a flank.*

To the Right (*or* Left), to—Paces, Extend.

The whole will form two deep. If the extension is to the right, the left man of the leading file will continue to advance, the other man of the file forming up on his right at the number of paces ordered. The remainder will make a partial turn in the required direction, and will double into their positions. The left man of each file will form on the left of the other man of the same file. As each man reaches his position he will break into quick time and continue to advance in the original direction.

If the extension is to the left, the right man of the leading file will continue to advance and the right man of each file will form on the right of the other man of the same file as above.

Note.—i. If, when working with two units, it is desired to extend outwards, one unit may be ordered to extend to the right, the other to the left.

ii. Should it be required to form in a direction oblique to the line of advance, the words *Half* (or *quarter*) *right* (or *left*) will precede the commands given above.

3. *Advancing.*

Advance.

If halted, the men will come to attention, and move

towards the objective, maintaining direction by the named
file.

Note.—If moving to a flank when the command is given,
they will turn to the right or left and advance towards the
objective.

If retiring, they will turn about.

4. *Halting.*

Halt.

The men will halt, face the objective, and stand at ease
(*See* Sec. 92, 4).

5. *Retiring.*

Retire.

The men will turn about, and if halted they will step off,
moving in the opposite direction to the objective.

6. *Changing direction on the march*

Change Direction—Right.

The man on the named flank will turn in the named direction and continue to move in quick time. The remainder will
form round at the double, breaking in to quick time when on
the new alignment. (*See* Sec. 92, 6.)

Note.—A change of direction *half right* (*or half left*) can be
made in a similar manner.

7. *Changing position (when halted).*

Change Position—Right.

The man on the named flank will turn in the named direction and stand at ease. The remainder will form round in
double time.

(B 10984)   E

8. *Inclining or turning.*

Right Incline ; *or* **Right Turn.**

The men act as in close order drill, the intervals between the men being preserved.

9. *Changing the pace from double to quick time, or vice versa.*

Quick Time ; *or* **Double.**

The men break into quick or double time, as ordered.

10. *An extended line closing.*

Close ; *or* **To—Paces, Close.**

The men will close on the centre, taking up their original positions in two ranks, or will decrease their extensions to the given number of paces. The front rank man of the centre file will stand fast, the remainder moving in quick time.

Notes.—i. If it is desired to close or decrease extensions towards a flank or on a named file, the above command will be preceded by the caution *On the right (or left)*, or *On No. —.*

ii. When troops are moving and it is desired to close and halt, the above command will be preceded by the caution *At the halt*, in which case the centre (right or left hand) man will halt, the remainder acting as above, and halting as they reach their places.

iii. If it is desired to close on the move the front rank man of the centre file will continue to advance in quick time, the remainder doubling to their places, and resuming quick time on arrival.

11. *Reinforcing (when two extended lines are being drilled in co-operation).*

Reinforce.

The rear or supporting line will double forward into the intervals of the. first or firing line, unless the reinforcement is directed on to a flank, which should be done when possible.

Note.—When a platoon or company is being exercised in extended order, subordinate commanders will be practised in the reorganization of units after reinforcement has taken place into the intervals of an extended line. Leaders will at once take command of the men in their vicinity, and the men will assist by placing themselves under the nearest officer or N.C.O.

After units have been reorganized in this manner they must, as far as possible, be re-formed under their original leaders on the first opportunity.

94. *Control and communication by signal.*

1. As soon as men have learnt how to drill when controlled by word of command, they will be taught how control can be exercised and communication maintained by means of the signals given below. As a preliminary measure, recruits should be formed up as for squad drill with intervals, and made to perform the various signals in unison, the instructor first giving the corresponding word of command or message and demonstrating the manner in which the signal should be made.

2. When controlling men by signal a " short blast " of the whistle (*i.e.,* " the cautionary blast," *see* Sec. **95**, 1) will first be blown, on which each man will look towards the instructor, who will then make the signal. When he is

satisfied that it is understood, the instructor will drop his
hand to the side, on which the men will act as ordered.
Signals should be made with whichever arm will show most
clearly what is meant.

3. The following " control signals " are used :—

Extend.—The arm extended to full extent over the
head and waved slowly from side to side, the hand
to be open and to come down as low as the hips on
both sides of the body.

Notes.—i. The above signal denotes *extend* (from
the centre). If it is required to extend to a flank,
the leader will point to the required flank before
dropping his hand.

ii. The number of paces to which men are to extend
will, unless prearranged, be communicated to the
nearest men by word of mouth and passed on by them.

Advance.—The arm swung from rear to front below
the shoulder.

Halt.—The arm raised at full extent above the head.

Retire.—The arm circled above the head.

Change direction, right (or left).—The arm is first
extended in line with the shoulder. A circular movement is then made, on completion of which the arm
and body should point in the required direction.

Notes.—i. When troops are halted, the above signal
means *change position, right (or left).*

ii. When troops are in column of fours, or in file
or single file, the above signal means *right (or left) wheel.*

Right (or Left) Incline.—The body or horse turned in

the required direction and arm extended in line with the shoulder, and pointing in the required direction.

Note.—There is no separate signal for the command *right (or left) turn*, but the "Incline signal" given twice in succession will effect the required movement.

Close.—The hand placed on top of the head, elbow to be square to the right or left according to which hand is used.

Notes.—i. The above signal denotes *Close* (on the centre). If it is required to close on a flank, the leader will point to the required flank before dropping his hand.

ii. If, when on the march, it is required to halt as well as close, the leader will perform the halt signal before dropping his hand.

Quick Time.—The hand raised in line with the shoulder, the elbow bent and close to the side.

Double.—The clenched hand moved up and down between the thigh and shoulder.

Reinforce.—The arm swung from rear to front above the shoulder.

Lie Down.—Two or three slight movements of the open hand towards the ground.

4. The following "communicating signals" are made with the rifle or other weapon.

Enemy in Sight in Small Numbers.—Weapon held up above, as if guarding the head.

Enemy in Sight in Large Numbers.—As for "Enemy in sight in small numbers," but the weapon raised and lowered frequently.

No Enemy in Sight.—Weapon held up at full extent of arm, point or muzzle uppermost.

95. *Control by whistle blasts and bugle calls.*

1. The following whistle blasts are used :—

The Cautionary Blast (a short blast).—To draw attention to a signal about to be made.

The Rally Blast (a succession of short blasts).—To denote close on the leader in wood, bush, fog or darkness, when the signal cannot be seen.

> *Note.*—On the above blast being given, the men will double towards the sound of the whistle, and will rally on the leader, facing in the same direction. If several units are being exercised, they will form up in close column, the leader marking the position of the right of the leading unit.

The Alarm Blast (a succession of alternate long and short blasts).—To turn out troops from camp or bivouac to fall in or to occupy previously arranged positions.

2. The only bugle calls used in war are the " Alarm " and the " Charge."

Note.—With a view to peace operations, all ranks should be made acquainted with the " Stand fast," the " Continue," and the " Dismiss."

96. *Control and communication by verbal messages.*

1. In the later stages of an action it will frequently occur that movements in extended order can no longer be controlled by whistle and signal without attracting the attention of the enemy. In these and similar circumstances it will often be necessary for orders and messages to be transmitted from

section commander to section commander, or even from man to man, by word of mouth.

2. The correct transmission of orders and messages by this method during the distracting influences of a battle is particularly difficult, and in order to attain proficiency it is important that all ranks should be given frequent practice especially during extended order drill, during field practices, and whenever blank ammunition is being used.

3. Orders and messages to be transmitted by this method must be as concise as is compatible with clearness. They must be passed as quietly as circumstances permit, and each word must be pronounced distinctly and deliberately. They must begin with the designation of the person for whom they are intended, and must end with the designation of the sender and the time of despatch; for instance, " To Commander No. 2 Section. Open fire on enemy near bushes 700 yards to your front. From Commander No. 1 Platoon, 3 p.m." It is forbidden to send a verbal order without saying from whom it emanates and for whom it is intended, *e.g.*, " Halt in front."

4. The recipient of a verbal order will acknowledge it by a salute if the sender is within view; if not, it must be acknowledged by a return message.

5. When the platoon or company is being exercised in extended order drill, individual men will be practised in carrying verbal messages direct from the issuer to the person addressed. The bearer of a verbal order or message should repeat it to the issuer and understand its purport. On approaching the addressee he should call out " Message for " and the name of the addressee in a loud tone. It is the duty of the senior present to direct the messenger. After receiving the message the addressee should repeat it to the bearer.

CHAPTER VI.

BATTALION DRILL.

97. *Preliminary remarks.*

1. Battalion drill is the combination of companies moving as in company drill. The aim of a battalion commander must be to obtain cohesion without rigidity, so that his companies may be able either to act as one body on his command or signal, or to move rapidly and, if necessary, silently into any formation required.

2. In the field, the movements of a battalion will usually be carried out in lines of platoons in fours, or in extended order.

A suitable formation of assembly for a battalion in the field is mass, or such modification of mass as may be dictated by the ground, the intervals and distances and the relative positions of the companies being regulated according to circumstances. In such a formation, or in lines of platoons in fours, the battalion can either be manœuvred on the executive word or signal of its commander, or the companies can rapidly be shaken out into any more open formation required.

Battalion drill will therefore usually consist of movements in mass and in lines of platoons in fours at varying intervals and distances, and from mass into column of fours and *vice versa.* Company commanders will be practised in carrying out their commander's orders rapidly and silently in the manner described in Sec. 88, and in meeting unexpected emergencies as the situation may require. The guiding principle is that though, to secure precision in close order drill, executive commands must be given by platoon

PLATE XV.   *To face p.* **93.**

A BATTALION IN MASS.

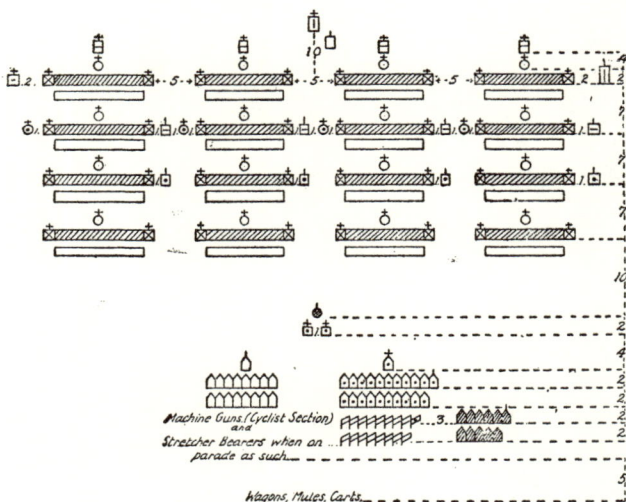

Machine Guns (Cyclist Section)
and
Stretcher Bearers when on
parade as such

Wagons, Mules, Carts.

— Key. —

Battalion Commander.	Platoon Commander.	Staff Serjt {Regtl Q.M.S. / Armourer	Band Serjt.
Senior Major.	Quartermaster.	Platoon Serjeant.	Bandsman.
Adjutant	Serjeant Major.	Section Commander.	Serjt Drummer.
Company Commander.	Company Serjt Major.	Pioneer Serjeant.	Drummer.
2nd in Command.	– do – Q.M.S.	Pioneer	Signalling Serjt.
		Bandmaster.	Signaller.

as well as company commanders, movements in the field should, whenever possible, be carried out on the word **Move** or pre-arranged signal, words of command being reduced to an absolute minimum.

Battalions will also be exercised in formations applicable to operations against ill-armed enemies* (*see* Sec. **100**).

98. *General rules.*

1. For battalion drill a battalion will usually form up in mass.

2. In mass, when platoons are of unequal strength, the inner flank of each company will be at five paces interval from the outer flank of the strongest platoon of the company next to it.

3. The battalion commander will place himself where he can best exercise supervision ; the adjutant will usually accompany him.

The position of the senior major in mass is beside the guide on the directing flank of the platoon of direction.

The normal positions of officers and warrant officers, and of battalion headquarters and the machine-gun section, in mass, are shown on Plate XV.

4. After forming mass on the left the right will be named as the directing flank, and *vice versa.*

5. When in column of route, pioneers and signallers will lead the battalion. Drums and band will be 20 paces in front of the leading company, or, if desired, either, or both, may be in the centre of the column ; machine guns, stretcher bearers, ammunition animals, carts, and wagons will be in rear of the battalion ; the whole in the above order. The

---

*Not applicable to Special Reserve and Territorial Force.

cyclist section, in the case of units which have one, will be in rear of the machine guns. The machine-gun detachments will march in rear of the limbered wagon or of the pack animals, carrying the guns. In no case should more than four men march abreast, including commanders and supernumeraries. The adjutant will accompany the battalion commander, who will be at the head of the leading company. The senior major will be in rear of the battalion. The serjeant-major will be in front of the leading company.

6. A column of route will always march by the left and will march on the left side of the road unless direct orders to the contrary are issued. In the event of the men who are marching on the extreme left of the road being caused greater inconvenience than the others, the relative positions of the men in each section of fours may be changed from time to time. The distances to be maintained between battalions and companies on the march are 20 yards and 10 yards respectively, and will be reckoned from the rear officer or man of one battalion or company to the leading dismounted officer or man of the next.

7. The positions of officers, &c., in para. 5 do not apply to movements on or near the battlefield, where the battalion commander is responsible that his battalion is arranged to suit the tactical requirements. For instance, it may be necessary to place the machine guns in front of the battalion and the serjeant-major may be in charge of the ammunition. It will often be important that all the company commanders should be in advance of the battalion to reconnoitre ground, to receive instructions, or to select methods for passing their companies over obstacles on the line of march.

93. *Movements from and into mass.*

1. *A mass advancing.*

The Battalion will Advance, Quick—March.

The men will move as in squad drill. The right will direct unless otherwise ordered.

2. *A mass moving off in lines of platoons in fours.*

Move to the Right in Fours, Form—Fours, Right. Quick—March.

The men will move as in squad drill, preserving the intervals and distances between platoons and companies. The left will direct unless otherwise ordered, each leading four of the outer platoons of each company dressing by the leading four of the platoon on its left.

Note.—From this formation the companies can be opened out to varying distances and intervals, with irregular frontages, as the battalion commander may direct.

3. *A mass moving off in column of fours.*

Advance (or Retire) in Fours, No. — Company Leading.

The commander of the named company will give : *No. — Form—Fours, Right (or Left)*. The commander of the leading (or rear) platoon will then give *Left (or Right) Wheel, Quick—March*, and the remaining platoons of the company will be marched off by their commanders in succession in the same way. The remaining companies will successively be marched off in the same way in time to follow the preceding company.

4. *A column of fours forming mass facing in the same direction.*

At the Halt, on the Left, Form Mass.

The commander of the leading platoon will at once give *At the halt, on the left, form platoon.* Each platoon commander of the leading company will act similarly when his leading guide reaches close column distance from the platoon in front. The remaining companies will disengage to the left, and will be led to their respective positions in mass, where close column of platoons will be similarly formed.

Notes.—i. Mass can similarly be formed on the right.

ii. Any modification of mass may be formed in a similar manner (*see* Sec. **97, 2**).

5. *A column of fours forming mass facing a flank.*

At the Halt, Facing Left, Form Mass.

The commander of the leading platoon will at once give *Halt, Left—Turn.* The remaining platoons of the leading company will be led by the shortest route to their position in close column of platoons, where they will receive a similar command.

As the leading platoon of each succeeding company arrives at the correct interval from the preceding company, close column of platoons will be formed in a similar manner.

Note.—Any number of lines of platoons in fours can be formed from column of fours on the above principle, the platoon commander's command *Left—Turn* being omitted. The battalion commander's caution will be **At the Halt, on the Left, Line (or — Lines) of platoons in fours, at — paces interval (and — paces distance).**

PLATE XVI.   *To face p. 97.*

BATTALION DRILL.

Formations applicable to operations against ill-armed enemies.

Fig. 1.
Open Ma⁗⁄

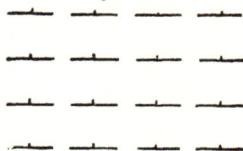

Fig. 2.
Echelon Outwards.

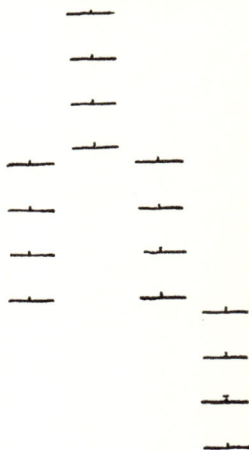

Fig. 3.
*Double Column of Platoons at
deploying interval.*

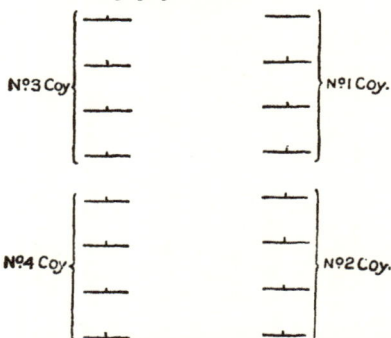

Nº3 Coy.

Nº1 Coy.

Nº4 Coy.

Nº2 Coy.

*Note.—In deploying to the front, No. 2 will be on the
right of No. 1, and No. 4 on the left of No. 3. Similarly,
when line is formed facing left, No. 1 will be on the right
of No. 3, and No. 2 on the left of No. 4.*

100. *Formations applicable to operations against ill-armed enemies.*

The object to be aimed at when manœuvring against ill-armed enemies is to move the battalion in a formation from which a fire front in close order can be rapidly and steadily presented in any direction.   No stereotyped formations can be laid down for these occasions, it being essential that the battalion should be manœuvred in the manner most suitable to the ground and local conditions ; but the elasticity of open mass (line of columns of platoons) makes this a convenient basis for all subsequent movements.   From this formation the companies can be opened out to deploying interval ; or they can be echeloned from the right or left, or outwards ; or the battalion can advance in column, or double column, of platoons (*see* Plate XVI), from all of which formations a fire front of two or more companies as required can readily be presented.

The battalion should be practised in moving into these various formations rapidly and steadily, according to the principles laid down in Sec. **97** (2), on the battalion commander's command **Echelon from the right (or left), or Outwards, Form—Echelon ; Advance in column of platoons, No. —** company leading ; or **Advance in double column of platoons Nos. — and — companies leading.**

Movements in echelon are especially useful when it is necessary to be prepared for attack from an oblique direction, or when attack by cavalry is probable.

CHAPTER VII.

DRILL OF THE MACHINE GUN SECTION.

101. *Elementary training.*

1. The elementary training of the machine gunner will be carried out as directed in Sec 8.

He must be taught at an early stage to hold the gun so that sufficient pressure is applied to the handles to check its vibration without transferring the vibration to the mounting.

Machine guns vary considerably and such variations can only be counteracted by a thorough knowledge of the particular gun and by skilful holding. Whenever the gun is laid, the holding should be such as would be employed in actually firing service ammunition. This can only be judged by the man himself, but it should be impressed upon him that the habit of good holding is most important.

2. An early opportunity should be taken to demonstrate the necessity for correct holding. This may be done by a trained number firing a few rounds of ball ammunition at 30 yards range with different pressures on the handles.

3. During this elementary training, untrained numbers should attend on any occasion when firing is being carried out. They should also be present when the gun is stripped by the armourer.

102. *Allocation of duties.*

1. The duties of the section officer are to command his section in accordance with his orders and the tactical situation; to select gun positions, to observe, and to control fire

generally ; to regulate the ammunition supply, and to give instructions regarding the movement of unlimbered wagons. When guns are brigaded, he acts under the instructions of the brigade machine gun officer, watches for signals, and acts as the brigade machine gun officer may direct.

2. The duty of the serjeant is to supervise guns coming into action as the section officer may direct. He must be prepared to take command of the section in the event of the officer becoming a casualty.

3. The corporal is generally responsible for the packing and contents of the limbered wagon. On the line of march he marches behind it and works the brake as required. On the order to unpack he will lower the tail board, superintend the unpacking, and take command in the absence of the section officer or serjeant. He will see that Nos. 4 put their own rifles as well as those of Nos. 1, 2, and 3 in the wagon. He will have the spare parts box handy, supervise the ammunition supply and filling of belts, direct the limbered wagon as required, superintend the filling of sandbags and cutting of brushwood, and watch for signals from the section officer. He will be prepared to take the place of the serjeant should he become a casualty.

4. The following are the duties of the various numbers :—

No. 1, is the firer. He will personally clean and look after his gun and ensure that the mechanism is working smoothly. On going into action he will carry the tripod and place it in a suitable position and assist No. 2 in mounting the gun. He repeats all orders received, observes his own fire, and makes necessary alterations of elevation and direction.

No. 2, assists No. 1 at the gun, carries the gun into action, and mounts it with the assistance of No. 1. In action he will attend to the feeding of the gun, watch for signals from the section or brigade machine gun officer, and generally assist No. 1.

Nos. 3 and 4, are ammunition carriers. No. 3 takes the first supply of ammunition to the gun, assisted by No. 4, and arranges that the spare parts wallet is brought up to the gun position. No. 4 takes the ammunition from the limber to No. 3, when a further supply is required, and also the condenser complete and half-filled with water. No. 3 is responsible that the condenser reaches the gun position before there is any chance of the water boiling. No. 4 places his own rifle and those of Nos. 1, 2, and 3, in the limber.

No. 5, acts as scout, as ordered by the section officer.

One No. 6 is the range taker. He will take ranges and prepare range cards. (*See* Plate XVII.) The other No. 6 is a spare man and acts according to the orders he receives from his officer.

5. In allotting the various duties, section officers should select the men who show a particular aptitude for each duty, and the next best should be those who would probably be most quickly available on service to replace a casualty. The results obtained in Table " C," in Range Takers' Tests, and in Tests in Belt filling, will assist section officers in detailing the numbers, and for this purpose they will keep careful record of the characteristics and particular aptitude of each man. Nos. 1, 2 and 3 should be the best in that order of merit at laying and holding, Nos. 5 and 6 at range taking, and No. 4 at belt filling. In peace, the numbers should frequently change round, so that each may be trained in the duties of all numbers under various conditions.

The serjeant should similarly be practised in the duties of section officer and the corporal in the duties of serjeant.

PLATE XVII.

To face p. 100.

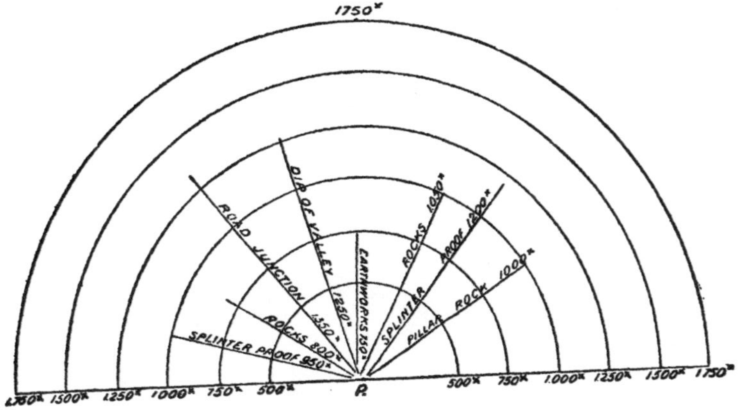

1750ʸ

EARTHWORKS 150°

DIR OF VALLEY 1250°

ROAD JUNCTION 1350°

SPLINTER PROOF 800°

ROCKS 900°

SPLINTER ROCKS 1630°

ROCKS 1680°

PILLAR ROCK 1650°

250ʸ 500ʸ 750ʸ 1000ʸ 1250ʸ 1500ʸ 1750ʸ

250ʸ 500ʸ 750ʸ 1000ʸ 1250ʸ 1300ʸ

O

6. *Signall.ng.*—Machine gunners should have a thorough knowledge of semaphore, and should pass periodical tests.

103. *Section drill, without transport.*

1. The guns, with tripod and ammunition boxes, will be placed on the ground, muzzles to the front and in line, legs to the rear, straps lapped round the rear leg and buckled, and clamps sufficiently tight to prevent the legs from hanging loose when the tripod is lifted off the ground ; the traversing clamp should be sufficiently loose to enable the gun to be deflected by a sharp tap with the hand on the rear cross-piece ; guns on the right, ammunition boxes 3 paces in rear of the guns. The guns should be a convenient distance apart, but not closer than 8 paces.

2. On the command **Fall In** the detachments for the two guns will fall in in two ranks, 5 paces in front of the interval between the guns ; the serjeant on the left of the front rank, covered by the corporal in the rear rank. The front rank will provide the right gun detachment, the rear rank the left gun detachment.

On the command **Number** the section will act as in Sec. **29.**

On the command **Take Post**, detachments turn outwards and double to their respective guns (the serjeant and corporal on the outer flank, where they can superintend). Nos. 1 and 2 fall in on the left of the tripod and right of the gun respectively, No. 3 on the left of the ammunition box. If the ground is suitable, these numbers should lie down.

Nos. 4, 5 and 6 fall in, in single rank, in rear of No. 3.

3. A landscape target should be placed about 25 yards from the guns. The instructor having pointed out a spot, not more than 5 yards away from where the guns are lying, where each gun will be mounted, will give the command

Mount gun. No. 1 picks up the tripod, having previously
seen that both elevating screws are exposed the same distance,
carries it to the spot ordered, and places it in position.   In
adjusting the tripod, he must ensure that the cross head
is upright, and that the legs are clamped tight.   He
must learn by experience the adjustment that suits him
best for the position ordered and for the nature of the ground,
so that he will not be cramped when firing and will not have
to alter the tripod after the gun has been mounted.

As soon as the tripod is nearly in position, No. 2 picks up
the gun and carries it to the right side of the tripod, holding
the rear cross piece with the left hand, with the gun muzzle
to the rear, under the right arm.   He then kneels on the left
knee, facing the tripod, and, supporting the weight of the
gun on the right knee, places it on the tripod, drives in and
turns down the cross head joint pin, and removes the cork
plug from the steam escape hole.   No. 1 fixes the elevating
joint pin, and directs the gun towards the mark.   Meanwhile,
No. 2 kneels and places the ammunition box in position.

No. 2 should time his advance so as to reach the tripod
at the moment its adjustment is completed.

When No. 3 sees the gun is nearly mounted, he carries the
ammunition box forward and places it within reach of No. 2.
The ammunition must be at hand directly No. 2 is ready for
it.   No. 3 then retires to a position not immediately in rear
of the gun.

4. On the command **Load**, No. 1 at once raises the tangent
sight, No. 2 passes the tag of the belt through the feed block.
No. 1 turns the crank handle on to the buffer spring, and with
his left hand pulls the belt straight through to the left front
as far as it will go, and lets go the crank handle ; he releases
the strain on the belt, then turns the crank handle on to the

buffer spring ; he again pulls the belt to the left front and
lets go the belt and crank handle. The gun is now loaded
and ready to fire. Each motion should be distinct and clean.

5. On the command (range), *e.g.*, **900**, No. 1 repeats the
order for his own gun, and adjusts the slide to the elevation
required for the distance ordered.

6. On the command **At** ———— (naming the aiming mark),
No. 2 adjusts the traversing clamp if told to do so by No. 1,
and No. 1 lays the gun, maintaining the same pressure on
the handles while laying as he would when firing.

7. When the gun is laid No. 1 raises the automatic safety
catch with the forefinger, and prepares to fire. When No. 1
is ready, No. 2 holds up his hand. As proficiency increases
the pause between naming the range and the aiming mark
should be slight.

8. On the command **Fire,** No. 1 presses the double button.

9. On the command **Cease Fire,** No. 1 releases the automatic
safety catch. and remains steady.

10. *Traversing fire.*—Frequent instruction will be given in
traversing fire. (*See* Sec. **163.**) The firer must first ensure
that the traversing clamp is just sufficiently loose to enable
the gun to be deflected by means of a sharp tap with the hand
on the rear cross piece. Each man must learn by experience
the exact degree of clamping he requires, and before firing
he should ensure that the clamp is correctly adjusted to suit
himself.

Traversing fire is applied by means of a series of groups
fired at regular intervals within certain limits indicated by
such figures on the target as may be ordered by the instructor.

The target will be the instructional machine gun target.

The procedure for horizontal traversing is as follows:—

The instructor having described the figure between which

fire is to be directed, will give the command **Traversing Fire.** The firer will lay the gun on the flank figure named and press the button, then tap the gun approximately to the centre of the interval to the next figure, again press the button, then tap and so on until the limit ordered has been reached. The firer should be taught to fire groups of about eight rounds by maintaining pressure on the button for about one second at each group. By this method he learns to tap the gun with the necessary force in order to avoid firing more than one group at the same place and also to avoid leaving gaps in the line he is traversing.

As proficiency increases instruction should be given in diagonal traversing. In this case the target will be three bands each with three figures as for horizontal traversing. The bands will be joined so that each of the outer bands is in the same vertical plane as the centre band and forms an angle of 120 degrees with it. In this case the firer is taught to combine the use of the elevating wheel with tapping for deflection. The same principles as for horizontal traversing apply for this diagonal traversing.

Instruction should be afforded in traversing from right to left as well as from left to right.

During the instruction fire should be stopped at least twice in order to check the laying and also to measure the distance traversed. - By comparing the distance traversed with the number of groups fired, an estimate can be deduced as to the value of the traversing fire. For example :— Traversing fire is ordered from the 1st to the 6th figure ; fire is stopped after the 4th group. If the traverse has been correctly carried out the gun should be laid on the interval between the 2nd and 3rd figures.

11. On the command **Unload**, No. 1 lowers the tangent

sight but not the slide, turns the crank handle twice in succession on to the buffer spring, letting it fly back each time on to the check lever ; then presses up the finger pieces on the lower pawls, while No. 2 withdraws and repacks the belt in the box ; this must be done correctly and the lid closed and fastened ; No. 1 clears the ejector tube and lock, and releases the lock spring by pressing the double button.

8. On the command **Dismount gun**, No. 1 removes the elevating joint pin, No. 2 replaces the cork plug, passes the ammunition box to No. 3, removes the gun as in mounting, and replaces it in its original position in rear.   No. 1 follows with the tripod.   On reaching the original position, he sees that the joint pins are home and turned down, and then folds and clamps the legs.

9. Instruction should be afforded in bringing the gun into action in the several positions of the tripod, and in various natures of ground.   Firing up, down, and along the side of steep hills should be practised.   Practice should also be afforded in mounting the gun from the prone position, in firing from the lying position, and when kneeling on both knees, as well as when sitting.

104. *Belt filling.*

1. The corporal, all the numbers, and also the drivers of the limbered wagon and S.A.A. cart when available, should be instructed and frequently practised in belt filling, both by hand and with the belt filling machine.*

---

*For description and method of using the belt filling machine, *see* the handbook of the gun.

105. *Drill with limbered wagons.*

1. The detachment will be formed up in two ranks six paces from the rear of the wagon facing outwards.

On the command or signal **Action,** the driver dismounts and stands to his horses. The serjeant and Nos. 5 and 6 double out to the section officer. The corporal lowers the tail board and superintends the unpacking. The remaining numbers ground arms on the word of command of the senior number and fall out to the wagon to perform the duties detailed in Sec. **102.**

The corporal selects a suitable covered position for the limbered wagon, if necessary.

2. On the command or signal **Dismount guns,** the procedure for unpacking is reversed and when completed, detachments fall in, and take up arms by word of command.

106. *Drill with pack transport.*

1. Normally mules will be led by Nos. 1, 2, 3, 4, 7 and 8. On the command **Prepare for action,** Nos. 2, 3, 7 and 8 will link their mules to those immediately in front of them. Nos. 7 and 8 will lead Nos. 1 and 4 mules, Nos. 1 and 2 will march on the tripod and gun sides respectively of No. 1 mule and loosen straps. Nos. 3 and 4 will march on either side of No. 2 mule.

2. On the command or signal **Action,** No. 1 will off-load the tripod and No. 2 the gun, No. 3 will off-load the leading ammunition animal. The corporal will select a suitable covered position for the pack animals. The other duties of the various numbers are as in Sec. **102.**

3. On the command or signal **Stand to,** Nos. 1, 2 and 3 will reverse the actions of off-loading. The detachment will then form up for marching.

CHAPTER VIII.

TRAINING IN FIELD OPERATIONS.

107. *General instructions.*

1. The previous chapters of this manual have dealt with the training of the infantry in close and extended order drill, the development of a soldierly spirit, and the inculcation of discipline. The following sections deal with training in the field, and with the application of the principles indicated in Field Service Regulations, Part I, and amplified in Part II of this manual. (*See also* Training and Manœuvre Regulations, Chap. III.)

2. In all stages of training advantage should be taken of local conditions to teach those lessons for which the nature of the ground is best suited.

3. In platoon and section training the men will first be exercised in the methods of attack and defence described in Part II, over as great a variety of ground as possible, and in the rudiments of outpost work. (*See* Chapter XIV.)

4. When the company commander considers that his platoons are fit to take their place in the company, the latter will be exercised as a whole.

5. The company commander will devote special attention to the training of platoon and section commanders in grasping situations rapidly, and in issuing clear and suitable orders quickly to their men. Special attention will also be devoted to the orderly continuance of operations after units have become mixed and commanders incapacitated (Sec. **93**, 11). Careful instruction will be given in the principles of wood and

village fighting, with practical illustrations where these can be arranged, and in the various duties of an outpost company.

6. Schemes for company training should be simple, and should usually deal with the various situations which would confront a company when operating with the remainder of a battalion.

7. In the later stages of company training it is important that situations should be worked out to their logical conclusion, and that troops should be practised in delivering and receiving an assault, in the pursuit, in assuming the offensive from the defensive, and in retirements. During this period a company should occasionally be made up to war strength by men of another company, in order to practise commanders in handling their units at war strength. At the end of the course the company should, when local conditions admit, carry out continuous training of about three days duration (*see* Training and Manœuvre Regulations).

8. Schemes for battalion training should deal with the situations which would confront a battalion acting as part of a brigade as well as a battalion acting independently. The battalion commander should pay special attention during this period to co-operation between his companies.

9. Whenever possible, arrangements should be made for cavalry, artillery, and engineers to co-operate with infantry during battalion training. If this is not possible the action and effect of these arms, and, in either case, the action and effect of air-craft, must be considered in the solution of tactical problems.

10. In peace operations, owing to fire effect being absent, and to the necessity for making a few rounds of blank last through hours of fighting, the tendency is to pay more attention to numbers, formations, and consequent vulnera-

bility of opposing forces than to fire direction, fire control, and fire discipline. It is of the highest importance to guard against this tendency, and all infantry commanders, at all periods of training in the field, should devote special attention to seeing that the principles of fire tactics are correctly taught and applied, so that neither bad habits may be acquired nor false lessons deduced from the more or less artificial conditions of peace operations.

11. Exercises in the field will be carried out under service conditions as regards equipment unless climatic conditions make this inadvisable.

12. Blank ammunition will be used in practising the more advanced exercises.

108. *Training in methods of advancing under fire, and in the use of ground.*

1. The soldier will be taught the importance of the relationship between fire and movement, and that the wise employment of every feature of the ground is of great importance in promoting fire effect and reducing losses. Special attention will be given to the various methods of advancing under different conditions of fire and ground, the conditions under which these methods are used being explained, while the one object of every advance, namely, to close with the enemy, is insisted on.

2. Platoon and section commanders will be taught that when an advance is being made by rushes, they should endeavour to decide beforehand on the next halting place, and should point it out to their men, who must get there as quickly as possible when the signal to advance is given.

3. Practical instruction will be given in the use of ground. The soldier will be taught that the most important

requirement in cover when firing is that he can use his rifle to the best advantage. In endeavouring to do so he should expose himself as little as possible to the enemy's fire, but must understand that if he merely seeks safety and neglects thereby the full use of his rifle he will be failing in his duty.

4. If an equally good view can be obtained it is better to fire round the side of cover than over it, as the firer is then less visible.

5. When firing from behind cover the soldier must keep his eyes on the target between each shot; otherwise he may lose sight of the target and this may result in his shooting without looking over the sights.

6. It will be explained that cover from view, which does not also afford cover from fire, should not provide a good aiming or ranging mark for the enemy. A hedge or bush, in country where such features are of uncommon occurrence, may become a dangerous trap if men crowd behind it and the enemy discovers they are there. Moving objects catch the eye more quickly than those that are still, and when, in default of cover, men are lying in the open, all but the necessary movements to load and fire must be avoided. Men halted in the open should not show up against the skyline.

7. Cover from hostile air-craft can best be obtained by moving through woods or along hedgerows. It will also be explained that the difficulties of observation from the air are increased if men stand still or lie down when a hostile air-craft approaches, and refrain from looking up when it passes overhead. It must be understood, however, that when once committed to the attack no attempt will be made by the firing line and supports to seek cover from the enemy's air-craft, the mission of which at this time will more probably be to locate the reserves.

8. It will be explained that even a few troops marching on a wide road are clearly visible from the air.   In order to conceal a movement from hostile air-craft troops should keep to the sides of the road, and march on grass rather than the metalled portion.   Narrow roads with high hedges are the most favourable for concealment.

109   *Training in field engineering and in duties in billets, camps, and bivouacs.*

1. Instruction will be given in the occupation and preparation of quarters (billets, camps, and bivouacs), *see* F.S. Regulations, Part I.   Men will be taught the importance of sanitation, and how to prepare food and to look after their own comfort in circumstances resembling as closely as possible those of active service (*see* Manual of Field Engineering).

2. Instruction will also be given in such field engineering as might be required to be undertaken by infantry in war. The soldier should have learned during the period of individual training how to use the various forms of tools, and the elementary principles of field fortification.   During his training in field operations he should be taught to apply his knowledge to various tactical situations, *e.g.*, attack, defence, protection, &c.   He should also be instructed in bridging expedients with materials usually available on service.

110. *Training in reconnaissance duties and instruction of scouts.*

1. All soldiers should be trained in reconnoitring, observing, and reporting the result of their observations.

2. One non-commissioned officer and four men in each company will in addition be specially trained as company scouts.

3. Infantry scouts work on foot, and usually operate near the force to which they belong.   When more extended

reconnaissance is required it will be carried out by mounted men or cyclists specially detailed for this purpose.

4. The value of the work done by scouts depends to a very great extent on the orders they receive before they are despatched on a particular duty. Every party of scouts sent out must have a particular objective assigned to it, and must be given specific questions to answer. The rôle of scouts is to observe and report, and when engaged on their special duties, they will only use their rifles in self defence.

5. The commander who despatches parties of scouts must arrange with them for means of rapidly communicating any intelligence gained.

6. During peace operations scouts should not be allowed to employ methods which would be impossible in war.

7. The training of scouts will be carried out principally during the period of individual training.

8. The methods to be adopted in the training of scouts are left to the officers concerned. The standard to be aimed at is that a scout should fulfil the following conditions :

(i) Know how to observe.

(ii) Be able to read a map easily.

(iii) Know what to report on, and how to make a report.

(iv) Be able to express himself clearly and concisely.

(v) Possess good sight and know how to use his eyes and ears.

(vi) Be self-reliant, resourceful, and prepared to take risks.

(vii) Understand semaphore signalling, and, if possible, be acquainted with all methods of visual signalling.

(viii) Thoroughly understand the use of ground ; be able to move about and see without being seen.

(ix) Be able to judge distance accurately and estimate numbers correctly.

(x) Be able to form sound conclusions from signs, such as clouds of dust, footprints, and so on.

(xi) Understand how to guide himself by compass, by the sun, and by stars.

(xii) Be of thoroughly sound physique and in good condition.

111. *Training in the conduct of infantry patrols.*

1. It will be explained that infantry patrols are used to obtain information of the enemy or of the ground in the vicinity of the force to which they belong. The strength of a patrol will depend upon the task allotted to it, and may consist of from two to eight men under an officer or non-commissioned officer.

2. The officer who sends out a patrol must give the patrol leader definite and precise instructions as to the points on which information is required. He must also inform him of the probable movements of other friendly troops in the neighbourhood and must tell him what is already known of the country in which he is to operate, the length of time he may expect to be away, and the place to which reports are to be sent.

3. After receiving his instructions, and forming his plan of action, the leader should explain the whole, or as much as may be desirable, to his subordinates, so that every man may know how to carry on the duty in the event of accidents. He should warn them that if captured they should refuse to give any information beyond stating their rank and name, and tell them that by international custom they cannot be punished for this refusal. No man should carry any written instruc-

(B 10984) F 2

tions or documents which would give information to the enemy.

4. Patrols should remember that their mission is not only to obtain information, but to convey it safely and quickly to the authority who sent them out. They should always endeavour, therefore, to move in such a formation that, if surprised, some of their number may be able to get back with the information gained. Their usual method of advance should be by bounds from cover to cover, every opportunity being taken to escape the notice of the enemy or of hostile inhabitants. They should keep as much as possible in the shadows, both by day and night. Any place likely to harbour an ambush, such as a wood, ravine, or village, through which it may be necessary to pass, must be approached with caution, one or two men advancing first under the cover of the rifles of the remainder. The whole party should never rest together in the same spot, but one or more look-out men should invariably be posted at these times.

5. An infantry patrol should seldom use its rifles if its object can be achieved by other means. But it must be clearly understood that if a small party of the enemy is suddenly encountered, the assumption of a resolute offensive will often be the best course of action.

6. Special points with regard to patrols sent out from an outpost line are discussed in Sec. **156.**

112. *Training in marching.*
(*See* Field Service Regulations, Part I, Secs. **24** to **33,** and Manual of Military Hygiene, Chapter VIII.)

1. The power of undertaking long and rapid marches without loss in numbers and energy is one of the chief factors of success in war.

The military spirit of troops is reduced by excessive fatigue ; fatigue can be reduced only by careful training.

2. Training in marching is begun during recruit training and must be carried out with care, especially in the case of recruits and men called up from the reserve, otherwise the training itself will result in a reduction in strength.

3. The recruit should not be trained in marching until he is so far advanced in his courses of drill and physical training as to know how to use his muscles and limbs properly.

4. Slow, gradual, and continuous progression is more important in this part of the soldier's training than in any other. Individuals must be carefully watched, faults in movement and in bearing must be corrected, and weaknesses in the different parts of the body must be removed by further physical exercises or by medical attention.

5. Before and during the training, instruction will be given in the fitting of socks, boots, and putties, the care of feet, cleanliness of body, &c.

6. The first marches during recruit training should be short, and marching order should not be worn, the chief object being to watch the movement and bearing of individuals. The distance should then be increased gradually, and the weight carried by the soldier brought up gradually to service marching order. After the period of individual training every trained soldier should be able to cover a long march in marching order. At the end of battalion training a battalion should be capable of undertaking a succession of long marches without loss in numbers.

7. In hot weather coats and shirts should be well opened at the neck and chest, and belts unbuckled. At the regular halts, and whenever else it is possible to do so, the 1908 pattern equipment will be removed. Men should also

be encouraged to lie down at the regular halts, and, if possible, to raise their feet, so as to relieve them of pressure and allow the blood to circulate.

8. Smoking, while actually marching, affects endurance, and should be discouraged.

9. The soldier should be taught that the sensation of thirst is aggravated rather than reduced by frequent recourse to his water-bottle, and endeavours should be made to develop a sense of self-discipline in this respect.

113. *Training in night operations.*

1. The chief object of this training is to accustom the soldier to moving in the dark, so that individuals and units can act with the same freedom by night as by day. The instruction will be begun during recruit training and will be carried out progressively ; it should culminate during the latter stages of company training and during battalion training in practice in the various methods of conducting night operations described in Field Service Regulations, Part I. The elementary work can be practised advantageously during winter afternoons and evenings. The more advanced exercises should be carried out late at night or in the early morning.

2. The elementary training should consist in explanations followed by practical work. The following may be taken as a general guide as to the methods to be adopted, only the more elementary being used in the training of recruits :—

(i) *Visual training.*—One man of a section should march away and be stopped by voice or pre-arranged signal as soon as he is out of sight. He should call out the number of paces he has taken. The same man should then advance towards the section from some distance further off, and be stopped as soon as he becomes visible, later counting his paces to the section.

It should be explained that :

   (*a*) Ability to see in the dark increases with practice.
   (*b*) Objects are more visible when the moon is behind the observer than when it is in front of him.
   (*c*) An observer may stand up when he has a definite background and should lie down when he has not.

When the men have been practised in observing a man approaching at a walk they should be similarly practised in observing a man who is endeavouring to approach unseen.

(ii) *Training in hearing.*—Instruction will be carried out on similar lines to visual training. At first the advance of a single man should be listened for, gradually the number should be increased so that facility may be acquired in judging the strength of a party approaching. It is easier to hear sounds on soft ground when standing, on hard ground when lying flat.

Listening should be practised on various types of ground, *e.g.*, open and enclosed country, across and in valleys, in woods, &c. The differences should be noted and explained.

(iii) *Silent advances.* At first individual instruction should be given to men without arms, later the company should be taken out in marching order and should practise advancing noiselessly on roads, and in various formations over open ground, with whispered words of command. The following rules should be observed :—

   (*a*) When moving in short grass or on hard ground the

toe should touch the ground first and the foot be raised higher than normally.

(b) In long grass the pace should be slow and the heel be placed on the ground before the toe.

(c) Precautions should be taken to prevent equipment rattling.

(d) Arms must not be allowed to clash against those of other men, and must be placed noiselessly on the shoulder and ground in sloping and ordering arms.

(iv) *Training in orientation.*—The training should be individual and conducted by means of questions. Men should be able to distinguish the Pole Star (or in the Southern Hemisphere the Southern Cross) and should also be instructed in the identification by night of natural objects as guides to direction.

(v) *Night firing.*

(vi) *Training of night sentries.*

(vii) *Reconnaissance prior to night advances and attacks.*— At first the point marking the objective for the night attack should be either some conspicuous object or should be marked by a flag. Men should not be allowed to approach nearer to the position than a point from which they might hope to avoid detection in daylight. From this point they should survey the line of approach to the objective by day. After dark, men, working in pairs, should advance on the objective from the point from which the reconnaissance was made by day. Men should be instructed in taking notes (written or mental) during the day reconnaissance, and should prior to the night work be questioned on the same. As proficiency increases the same procedure should be adopted with less conspicuous objectives.

(viii) *Entrenching at night.*—How to carry entrenching tools without making a noise ; the construction of various types of defences in the dark as silently as possible.   (*See* Manual of Field Engineering.)

(ix) *Intercommunication and verbal messages (see* Sec. **96**).— Messages should be passed in a whisper from front to rear, or *vice versa,* the final message received being checked with the original, in order to detect faults.

(x) *The system of protection on the march, and the best way of carrying it out in various types of country.*

PART II.—WAR.

CHAPTER IX.

INFANTRY IN BATTLE.

114. *General considerations.*

1. In no two military operations is the situation exactly similar. The character of the ground, the climatic conditions, the extent of the co-operation of the other arms, the strength and fighting spirit of the opposing forces, their physical condition, and the objects they wish to achieve must always differ.

It is impossible, therefore, as well as highly undesirable, to lay down a fixed and unvarying system of battle formations. General principles and broad rules alone are applicable to the tactical handling of troops in war.

2. The attitude originally assumed by either, or both, of the opposing forces, may be reversed during an engagement : a vigorous counter-attack by an army offering battle in a defensive position may throw the adversary on the defensive ; or an assailant may fight a delaying action in one part of the field. while in another part his action may be essentially offensive. These and all other variations in a combat, however, resolve themselves in every case into attack and defence, and it is under those headings that the action of infantry will be discussed in the two succeeding chapters.

3. The following sections of this chapter deal with general principles which apply to all stages of a combat, whether in attack or defence.

115. *Position and duties of commanders in action.*

1. During the fight, the commander of a considerable body of infantry influences the course of the action by means of his original orders and subsequently by the employment of his reserve.

2. The commander's position will, as a rule, be selected so that he can obtain an extensive view. It should be sufficiently central to facilitate the receipt of reports and the issue of orders. Brigade and battalion commanders and company officers will take post where they can best exercise supervision over their commands, watch the enemy, and receive and transmit orders.

3. In view of the importance of decentralization of command, it is essential that superior officers, including battalion commanders, should never trespass on the proper sphere of action of their subordinates. Personal example has undoubtedly an extraordinary influence, especially under heavy fire, and there are times when every other consideration must be sacrificed to leading or steadying the troops. But any attempt to exercise personal control over all portions of the force must inevitably lead to the neglect of other duties, such as feeding and supporting the firing line at the right place and time, protecting the flanks, meeting counterattacks, reporting to or communicating with the superior commander, and maintaining connection with the artillery and adjoining units.

116. *Fire direction and fire control.*

1. To obtain full value from the rifle, its powers and limitations must be understood, and its fire be applied with intelligence towards the object in view.

2. However skilful individual men may be, 'the greatest effect is produced by their fire only when it is efficiently directed and controlled. Fire is said to be **directed** by the commander who defines the objective against which it is to be used, and to be **controlled** by the fire-unit commanders who give the necessary executive words of command. In attack, occasions will frequently arise when fire-unit commanders must both direct and control the fire of their units, while at close ranges, or when men are widely extended, it may happen that the transmission of any fire order is impossible, and that each individual man must control his own fire.

3. The normal infantry fire-unit is the section, though under certain conditions at the longer ranges the fire of a platoon or even a whole company may be controlled by its commander. **The efficiency of section commanders is therefore of paramount importance.**

4. The value of a fire-unit commander depends upon his ability to apply the fire of his unit at the right time and in the right volume to the right target.

5. In addition to his other duties the fire-unit commander is responsible for :—

   (i) Indicating targets.
   (ii) Issuing orders for sighting, and, when possible, supervising the correct adjustment of sights.
   (iii) Regulating the volume of fire ; whether deliberate or rapid.
   (iv) Reporting when ammunition is running short.

6. When from his position it is possible for him to do so, the company commander decides as to the time for opening fire, subject to such orders as the battalion commander may issue, and regulates the supply of ammunition. In the defence he also normally arranges for the distribution or concentration of fire, and indicates the targets generally to his subordinates ; but in the attack these duties will usually devolve upon the subordinate commanders with the firing line.

7. In forming a decision as to when fire should be opened, the following considerations must have weight :—

(i) The early opening of fire discounts surprise and, whether in attack or defence, often indicates the positions of troops which would otherwise be unnoticed by the enemy. In attack it may unnecessarily delay the advance.

(ii) Beyond 1,400 yards the fire of even large and well controlled units of infantry has seldom much effect upon the decision of the struggle for superiority of fire. Exceptional circumstances, such as the appearance of considerable bodies of the enemy in vulnerable formations, may, however, justify the use of long range fire, especially in the defence (*see* below).

(iii) Between 1,400 and 600 yards, carefully controlled collective fire produces better results than the uncontrolled fire of individual men, which ceases to be sufficiently effective beyond ranges of about 600 yards to counterbalance the expenditure of ammunition involved.

8. Fire should therefore rarely be opened by infantry in attack when satisfactory progress can be made without it. The leading troops in particular should save every possible round for the final struggle for superiority of fire at close range, as the replenishment of ammunition in the firing line at that time will be a matter of considerable difficulty. When progress is no longer possible fire should be opened, either by such parts of the firing line as cannot advance, or by bodies of infantry specially detailed for this purpose, to enable a further advance to be made. Subject to these principles fire may be opened in attack when there is a probability of its producing good effect, or when withholding fire might lead to heavy loss.

9. When infantry is acting on the defensive, there is usually less difficulty in arranging for the supply of ammunition. Fire may therefore be opened at longer ranges than when attacking, if it seems probable that any advantage will be gained thereby, especially when it is desired to prevent the enemy coming to close quarters, and when the ranges have been ascertained beforehand. If, however, the object is to gain decisive results, it is generally preferable to reserve fire for closer ranges and for surprise.

10. It is usually necessary to keep the enemy's firing line under fire throughout its length in order to disturb his aim and prevent his movement, but against very vulnerable targets, or to produce an increased effect at a particular place, fire may be concentrated with advantage.

11. Oblique or enfilade fire has greater moral and material effect than frontal fire, for it comes usually from an unexpected direction and the target presented to it is generally more vulnerable. In defence, opportunities for the employ-

ment of enfilade fire may be created by careful pre-arrange-
ment between the commanders of adjoining units.

12. In deciding on the volume of fire to be directed against
the enemy at any particular time a commander should
consider chiefly the tactical situation, the target presented,
the effect it is desired to produce, the range, and the state
of the ammunition supply.

Fire should, as a rule, be delivered deliberately, each man
satisfying himself that every time he presses the trigger he
will hit the object aimed at.

**Rapid fire should be considered as a reserve of power
to be used when the occasion demands it.** It must
combine accuracy with rapidity, and never degenerate into a
wild expenditure of ammunition at the fastest possible rate.

Rapid fire may be required when it is necessary to beat
down the enemy's fire quickly ; when covering the withdrawal
of other troops ; when pursuing an enemy with fire ; when
meeting cavalry attacks ; or when good targets are exposed
for a very short period ; also, in attack, by all troops, as a
final preparation for the assault, and in defence to beat off
an enemy in the act of assaulting. The effect of surprise by
a sudden burst of accurate fire from an unexpected quarter
is very great. Short bursts of rapid fire, followed by pauses,
favour observation of results and give time for the adjustment
of sights. They also facilitate the control of fire in critical
situations. The duration of such bursts must be strictly
controlled, and limited to the requirements of the occasion,
for if rapid fire is continued for any length of time it
excites and exhausts the troops and leads to waste of
ammunition.

13. A sudden effective fire is known to have a particularly
demoralizing effect on the enemy ; it is often advantageous

therefore to seek for surprise effects of this sort by temporarily withholding fire.

14. Wild, unsteady fire causes little or no loss, and tends to encourage the enemy by inducing a belief in his mind that his opponent is shaken. It is therefore worse than useless against good troops.

15. Every available means should be used to obtain the correct ranges. Observers will be employed, as necessary, to assist in observation of fire, in watching the enemy and neighbouring troops, and in keeping up communication between platoons.

16. Observation of fire is the best means of ensuring that fire is effective. If uncertainty as to the elevation exists it is better to underestimate than to overestimate the range. If it is necessary to fire at ranges beyond 1,000 yards and observation has failed, or the situation requires that some effect should be produced quickly, combined sights may be employed, but satisfactory results will seldom be obtained by bodies of less than two platoons.

117. *Fire discipline.*

1. A high standard of fire discipline in the men is not less important than skilful direction and control of fire by the commanders.

Fire discipline means strict attention to the signals and orders of the commander, combined with intelligent observation of the enemy. It ensures the careful adjustment of the sight, deliberate aim, economy of ammunition, and prompt cessation of fire when ordered or when the target disappears.

It requires of the men endurance of the enemy's fire, even

when no reply is possible ; and a cool and intelligent use
of the rifle when superior control can no longer be exercised.

118. *Fire and formations in battle.*

1. The formations to be adopted in battle will depend
principally on the ground and the tactical situation.   In
order to avoid unnecessary loss in the attack, however, the
comparative effect of artillery and rifle fire on the various
formations at different ranges must be clearly understood by
all leaders. Similarly, if infantry in defence is to make the best
use of its ammunition, it must know what targets are most
vulnerable under the various conditions of the battlefield.

2. At effective ranges, troops advancing steadily and
rapidly suffer less than when they remain lying down, even
under moderately good cover.   This is due to the moral
effect on the enemy and to the constant alteration of the
range.   In retiring losses are always heavier than in
advancing.

3. Against frontal artillery fire, or direct long-range infantry fire, small shallow columns, each on a narrow front,
such as platoons or sections in fours or file, offer a
difficult target while admitting of efficient control, and
may be employed during the earlier stages of an attack.
These columns, making full use of the ground, should be on
an irregular front, so that the range from the enemy's guns
to each column is different, regard also being had to the forward
effect of shrapnel.

Infantry coming suddenly under artillery fire will usually
avoid loss more easily by advancing than by halting and
making use of cover, the position and range of which will
probably be known to the enemy.

4. Although serious effect from aimed infantry fire is not to be anticipated at ranges beyond about 1,400 yards, zones of considerable width, beaten by unaimed fire, may have to be crossed at such ranges. It is necessary that troops should be prepared for this and be ready to adopt formations which will reduce casualties. This applies, not only to firing lines and supports, but to reserves and other bodies in rear. Rifle fire at these long ranges has so steep an angle of descent that effective cover from it may be difficult to find.

5. On open ground swept by effective rifle fire an extended line is the least vulnerable formation, and on such ground it will usually be advisable to extend before it becomes necessary for the advancing troops to open fire. A formation in small columns should, however, be retained as long as it is applicable to the situation, for when once extended, a unit loses its power of manœuvre. As a general principle deployment is necessary when fire is to be opened, the amount of extension then depending on the volume of fire which it is required to produce, and upon the effect of the enemy's fire.

6. The greater the extension of a line, the fewer will be the casualties, but the less will be its fire effect. When the infantry struggle for superiority of fire has begun, casualties will be reduced, not so much by the formations in which the troops are disposed, as by the material and moral effect of their fire and, still more, of the fire of the artillery, machine guns, and infantry who are covering the movement.

7. The fire effect which infantry can develop against cavalry is such that infantry which is ready to open a steady and timely fire has nothing to fear from a cavalry charge, provided the cavalry cannot find dead ground over which to approach. Any formation which allows fire to be delivered quickly and accurately is suitable for meeting cavalry. Closing

an extended line to meet cavalry delays the opening of fire
and may offer a vulnerable target to the enemy's artillery.
Even if cavalry succeeds in riding through a firing line it
can inflict little loss upon it if the infantry holds its ground.
Whenever there is a possibility of being charged by cavalry,
special care must be taken to watch and guard the flanks.

8. Charges carried out by friendly cavalry will necessarily
distract the enemy's attention from the firing line of the
attack. The attacking infantry must take advantage of
such co-operation on the part of the cavalry by at once
pressing forward and gaining as much ground as possible.

9. Artillery coming into action, limbering up, or in movement, is a vulnerable target against which rapid fire or
even fire at long infantry ranges is justifiable. Infantry
will experience difficulty in putting shielded artillery out of
action by direct fire even at close infantry ranges, but it can
prevent the artillery from moving and interfere with the
service of the guns. Infantry can best obtain decisive effect
against guns with shields by means of enfilade or oblique
fire.

10. Machine gun sections with their guns on travelling
carriages are as vulnerable as artillery limbered up ; but
detachments carrying the gun into action are difficult to
distinguish from infantry. Machine guns in position are a
difficult target ; to obtain good effect against them it is
usually necessary to employ a considerable number of rifles.

11. Aircraft form a very difficult target to fire directed
from the ground, and only a small proportion of their area
is vulnerable. Bullets can pass through the fabric of aero-
plane wings without doing serious damage. Indiscriminate
fire at hostile aircraft is, moreover, likely to cause casualties in
neighbouring units, and will also disclose the position of the

troops to the enemy's observer. The strictest control must be exercised over all fire directed against aircraft. In the case of rifle fire at aeroplanes, men should be instructed to aim six times the length of the machine in front, and in the case of airships at the nose of the envelope.

119. *Intercommunication and passing of orders.*

1. All subordinate commanders are responsible for keeping their respective superiors, as well as neighbouring commanders, regularly informed of the progress of events and of important changes in the situation as they occur.

All ranks should notice what takes place within their view and hearing, and report anything of importance accurately and at once to their immediate superior, who must pass the information on to the higher commanders and to neighbouring units.

This is the foundation of co-operation in war and is essential not only in battle but at every stage of a campaign.

2. The senior in any body of troops is responsible for forwarding messages to their destination.

3. During an action every company commander will leave with the battalion commander one man of his company who can be trusted to carry a verbal message or order correctly and to describe intelligently the local situation. These men will be used to convey urgent orders to the companies in action, when this is possible.

Similarly battalion commanders will send a representative of his battalion to brigade headquarters during an action.

4. Within the battalion, orders and messages in battle will normally be verbal. Verbal initial instructions by a commander on the battlefield should conform generally to

the accepted type of written orders. They should give first such information of the enemy and his own troops as may be necessary, then his task and the general manner in which he intends to carry it out, and after that, detailed orders for the units at his disposal.

The importance of giving orders in a firm tone of voice and in a calm, determined manner cannot be exaggerated.

The passing of verbal orders and messages is to be reduced to a minimum owing to the liability of errors in transmission. In the firing line all verbal messages necessary must be passed as quietly as possible, as a rule from section commander to section commander. The fewer the individuals by whom the message has to be repeated, the less chance will there be of errors creeping in. (*See* Sec. **96.**)

5. Throughout an action all commanders should try to anticipate the various situations which may occur, and should decide what steps they would take to meet them. They will thus be better able, when the necessity arises, to issue orders promptly and with decision.

6. On a battlefield, when the ground is open, inter-communication between bodies of troops taking part in an attack becomes very difficult as soon as the enemy's fire is severely felt. Messengers may be unable to approach, and signalling may be impossible. In these circumstances co-operation is only secured by the watchfulness of the officers, especially those superintending the fight in any portion of the field. If officers are alert to act on indications expressed by the movement, or absence of movement, of their own troops or of the enemy, and if their tactical training has been conducted on sound and uniform principles, suitable action will follow in spite of the breakdown of positive methods of inter-communication.

120. *Artillery escorts.*

1. Artillery on the field of battle is generally protected by the distribution of the other arms. Batteries which have a clear field of fire can protect their own front; the flanks and rear of a line of guns are its most vulnerable parts.

2. Should the guns not be protected by the existing distribution of troops, a special escort should be detailed, and if this has not been done it is the duty of the artillery commander concerned to apply to the commander of the nearest troops, who must provide an escort. The duties of this escort will be :—

    (i) To give timely warning of any threatened attack.
    (ii) To keep hostile bodies beyond effective rifle range of the guns, or, in case of necessity, to cover the withdrawal of the guns.

3. All ground within rifle range which might afford concealment to an enemy should either be occupied by the escort or be under its effective fire. The escort commander should place himself where he can best superintend his command, and ensure rapid communication between himself and the artillery commander. The senior officer present, whether artillery commander or escort commander, will issue the necessary instructions to the escort, but the escort commander must in either case have a free hand in carrying them out.

CHAPTER X.

INFANTRY IN ATTACK.

121. *General considerations.*

1. As is explained in the Field Service Regulations, a commander who decides to take the initiative in forcing a decision usually divides his force into two parts ; the first part develops the attack, wears down the enemy's power of resistance by engaging him along his front and endeavouring to force him to use up his reserves, and thus prepares the way for the decisive blow to be struck by the second part, known as the General Reserve. The commander regulates the action of the two parts of his force chiefly by fixing their relative strength and preliminary position, by allotting their respective tasks, and by arranging for the correct timing of their movements in accordance with his general plan of battle.

2. When the commander of an attacking force has issued his orders it lies with the subordinate commanders to distribute the troops at their disposal in accordance with the tasks allotted to them.

Part of the infantry available will form *the firing line,* a portion of which will usually be kept back to form *supports.* Behind these will follow *local reserves* in the hands of battalion, brigade, and divisional commanders.

3. The relative strengths of these bodies will depend on the ground, the information available, time conditions, and the possibility of effecting a surprise. Each portion of the firing line will be given a definite objective or task, and it may also be advisable to fix the limits of its flanks.

4. As much as possible of the line of advance must be reconnoitred beforehand. In close country this will be carried out by officers or scouts ; in open country it may be necessary to depend on observation through field glasses. It will usually be found, as a result of such reconnaissance, that certain lines of advance afford better concealment than others, while the localities offering the best facilities for covering fire will be brought to notice.

5. The main essential to success in battle is to close with the enemy, cost what it may. A determined and steady advance lowers the fighting spirit of the enemy and lessens the accuracy of his fire. Hesitation and delay in the attack have the opposite effect. **The object of infantry in attack is therefore to get to close quarters as quickly as possible,** and the leading lines must not delay the advance by halting to fire until compelled by the enemy to do so.

6. **The object of fire in the attack, whether of artillery, machine guns, or infantry, is to bring such a superiority of fire to bear on the enemy as to make the advance to close quarters possible.**

7. The action of infantry in attack must therefore be considered as a constant pressing forward to close with the enemy. Owing to the effect of the enemy's fire, however, this onward movement can rarely be continuous, and when effective ranges are reached there must usually be a fire-fight, more or less prolonged according to circumstances, in order to beat down the fire of the defenders. During this fire-fight the leading lines will be reinforced ; and as the enemy's fire is gradually subdued, further progress will be made by bounds from place to place, the movement gathering renewed force at each pause until the enemy can be assaulted with the bayonet.

8. When the ground permits, it is generally necessary to detail special detachments of infantry to provide covering fire for the leading troops. These detachments will usually be detailed from local reserves in the original distribution for the attack, but any commander, at any stage of the fight, may detail troops from those under his command to assist his advance. No fire-unit commander, however, is justified in abandoning, on his own initiative, an advancing *rôle* in order to become a detachment for covering fire.

In undulating or mountainous country it may be possible for these detachments to cover the advance from positions in rear, but in flat country it is impossible for infantry or machine guns to fire over the heads of their own troops, and opportunities for supplying covering fire must be sought on the flanks. (*See* Sec. **116**, 11.)

Troops detailed to give covering fire to others must take care to select as targets those bodies of the enemy whose fire is chiefly checking the advance. Great difficulty will often be experienced in detecting which these are, and all ranks must be on the alert to notice any indication of their presence.

As soon as their fire ceases to be effective in aiding the advance of the firing line, it is the duty of troops detailed to give covering fire at once to join in the advance, unless definite orders to the contrary have been received.

9. During the advance, all important tactical points gained, such as suitable buildings, small woods, &c., should, when required, at once be put in a state of defence, so that the enemy may not be able to recapture them and that they may serve as supporting points to the attack. Local reserves will often find opportunities for strengthening localities gained by the firing line, and to assist them in this work.

detachments of engineer field companies may be attached
to them with advantage.

10. Infantry when advancing must be careful not to interfere with the fire of guns in action. A line of guns should be
passed on the flanks, or in the intervals between batteries and
brigades.   If it is unavoidable that infantry should pass
through guns, it should do so at the double.   Infantry ceases
to mask the fire of artillery about 500 yards in front of the
guns on level ground.

11. During the later stages of an attack the replenishment
of ammunition in the firing line by individuals will be practically impossible, and all reinforcing troops must be provided
with extra rounds for the men in front.

12. When the advancing line is checked by a heavy and
accurate fire, it will become necessary to continue the advance
by rushes, which, according to the ground and the proximity
of the enemy, will be made by the whole line simultaneously
or by portions of it alternately.

The length of rushes must depend upon the ground, the
enemy's fire, and the physical condition of the troops.   It is
often advisable to make a rush of some length across open
ground in order to reach good cover behind which men can
rest.   Similarly, if a firing line finds a long downward slope
devoid of cover, it is often best to make one rush to the bottom
of the slope.

In advancing by rushes within close infantry range the
particular portions of the line to move first, and the strength
of each such portion, will be determined partly by the ground
and the enemy's fire, but chiefly by the **resolution and determination of the various leaders in the front line.**   It
must therefore be the principal aim of every leader in the
front line to get his command forward.   Rushes should be

as strong as is reasonably possible. Creeping and advancing man by man check the rate of progress and are to be regarded as exceptional methods, only to be employed when it is impossible to gain ground in any other way.

13. Infantry in attack must not delay the advance or diminish the volume of fire by entrenching. Entrenchments in the attack are only used when, owing to further advance being impossible, the efforts of the attacking force must temporarily be limited to holding the ground already won. The advance must be resumed at the first possible moment.

14. Whenever a subordinate artillery commander is allotted a task necessitating co-operation with a certain force of infantry, whether he is placed under the orders of that force or not, it becomes his duty to open communication with its commander, reporting to him in person if possible, in order to obtain full information as to the character of the operation that he is to support, and as to the proposed method of its execution. The best results will be obtained when the artillery commander is able to discuss the situation with the infantry commander before the operation begins, but if this is not possible, or if he cannot remain with the infantry commander, he should be represented by an artillery officer. It is the duty of the infantry commander concerned, once communication with the artillery has been opened, to assist in its maintenance throughout the operation. It is unsafe to rely on one means of communication only, and two, or even more, should usually be arranged.

15. For the purpose of directing the fire of his batteries against what are, for the time being, the most important targets from the infantry point of view, the information which is of primary importance to the artillery commander is the exact positions of the infantry which he is supporting,

its immediate objective, and the cause which is preventing it from reaching this objective.

16. Quick-firing guns cannot maintain a rapid fire throughout a battle. Artillery use rapid fire when the infantry firing line is seen to be in need of assistance to enable it to advance ; infantry must take every advantage of periods of rapid artillery fire to gain ground.

17. In communications between infantry and artillery the mutual adoption of some system of describing the features of the ground, such as squared maps or panorama sketches, will often save delay and misunderstanding.

18. If the enemy is surprised it is of the utmost importance to increase the demoralization which the surprise will have already produced by pressing forward with the greatest energy. In such conditions the gradual building up, by means of successive reinforcements, of a powerful firing line, should be discarded, and the firing line should be strong from the first. A portion of the attacking force should, however, be retained temporarily in reserve to meet counter-attacks and unforeseen emergencies.

122. *The battalion in attack.*

1. A battalion forming part of the force launched to the attack will be divided by its commander into (1) firing line and supports ; (2) local reserve. The relative strengths of these two parts will depend on the task allotted to the battalion and on the ground. When the ground permits a portion of the battalion will usually be detailed as special detachments to provide covering fire (*see* Sec. **121**, 8).

2. If, owing to the presence of other units on the flanks, a definite frontage as well as an objective is allotted to the

battalion, it should be occupied lightly, though not necessarily continuously, from the outset.

3. When more than one company is detailed for firing line and supports it is advisable that each company so detailed should be represented in the firing line from the outset and should have a definite portion of the battalion's objective allotted to it. The maintenance of control and command will thus be facilitated by each company being distributed in depth rather than in breadth, and the inevitable mingling of units will be delayed and reduced.

4. The powers of personal control of a battalion commander upon the field of battle are limited, and success will depend, in a great measure, on the clearness of the order which commits his leading companies to the attack, and the definite objectives which he gives to each company in the original firing line. It is of importance, therefore, that the battalion should not be hurried into action without good reason, but that time should be taken for a survey of the ground, for the issue of orders, and for instructions to be given by company commanders to their subordinates and to the men.

When time permits company commanders and the commander of the machine gun section should be assembled at a point where as much as possible of the ground to be passed over during the operation is visible, and each must be informed, not only of his objective and of what part he is to play, but also of the objectives of the other companies, and those of other portions of the force in their neighbourhood. It will generally be useful to take advantage of this opportunity to point out to rangetakers the objectives of an attack, and to have ranges taken and noted When the objectives cannot be seen from the spot where the orders are issued, their direction should be stated by reference to a map.

Company commanders will act on similar principles in issuing orders to their subordinates.

Occasions will, however, constantly arise in war when instant action is imperative. All commanders and bodies of troops must therefore, when in the neighbourhood of the enemy, be prepared to dispense with preliminaries and to act at a moment's notice. (*See* Sec. **133** (2) and **136** (2).)

5. Next to the conception of a sound plan of attack, and the issue of clear and comprehensive orders to the company commanders, the most important duty of a battalion commander is the handling of his local reserve. It is by means of this reserve that he makes his influence felt in action. By providing covering fire by means of special detachments, or by reinforcing the firing line at the right time and at the right place, he keeps the attack moving and eventually attains superiority of fire. But judicious support to the firing line is not all that is required. Not only must its flanks be protected, if exposed, and its advance be supported by fire, but if the enemy is well trained, counter-attack is to be apprehended, or a sudden reinforcement of the defence may take place when the struggle for fire superiority is at its height. It should be the aim, then, of the battalion commander so to regulate the employment of his local reserve, that while prosecuting the attack with vigour by means of timely reinforcements, he may still have a sufficient force at his disposal to deal with any unexpected developments. He should, therefore, retain at least a portion of the reserve in his own hand as long as possible.

The battalion commander must not, however, fail to throw in reserves at any time when it appears to him necessary to do so during the advance, and in any case, when the moment for decisive action has arrived, every man must be used to complete the enemy's overthrow. Stragglers and slightly wounded men should be collected and formed into reserves whenever met with.

6. The formations in which the local reserve should advance must depend upon the ground and upon the probable effect of the enemy's fire at various ranges. In deciding this question the commander will be guided by the general principles contained in the preceding sections, the object being to get the reserve forward with the least premature expenditure of its fighting energy. The commander of the reserve will, when time permits, take steps to have the ground over which he is to pass reconnoitred before each advance.

7. For the duties of the machine-gun section, *see* Sec. **158,** *et seq.*

123. *The company in the firing line.*

1. The orders which the company commander will issue before advancing to the attack will be based primarily on those received from his battalion commander, and secondly, on the reports of scouts, on his personal reconnaissance of the ground, and his knowledge of the situation. He should make full use of his horse during the preliminary stages, to reconnoitre ground and to keep in touch with his battalion commander and adjacent companies.

2. The company should, as a rule, be divided into firing line and supports, and, if operating alone, a reserve should be kept in hand as long as circumstances permit.

3. In formulating his orders the company commander should indicate generally the task, objective, and direction of each platoon. If more than one platoon is detailed for the

initial firing line, he should allot a definite objective to each. He must arrange for the replenishment of ammunition, and decide on the position of the ammunition animals during the advance. He should inform his officers of the place to which reports are to be sent and of his own position during the earlier stages of the operation.

4. If considered desirable, a few scouts may precede the firing line before fire is opened, to feel the way for the advance. They should be sufficiently far in advance of the firing line and of the exposed flank of the company to obviate surprise and to obtain timely information as to the ground which the company is to cross. In close or undulating country connecting files may be necessary to maintain touch with the scouts, but they should be recalled as soon as connection can be maintained without them. Scouts preceding the firing line will, when checked, remain in observation until the firing line comes up to them, when they will rejoin their companies. Scouts on the flanks will remain in observation and keep connection with other units on the flanks until recalled.

5. When once the firing line comes under effective fire its further advance will be assisted chiefly by the covering fire of artillery, machine guns, and special detachments of infantry detailed for the purpose, and every advantage of this covering fire must be taken by all attacking troops to gain ground.

6. The various portions of the firing line will also on occasions be able to afford each other mutual support by fire, and all commanders must be on the alert to assist units on their flanks in this manner when the situation requires. Mutual support in the firing line will, as a rule, however, be more automatic than deliberately arranged, and in no case must its employment be allowed to induce

h?sitation in the advance. The paramount duty of all leaders in the firing line is to get their troops forward, and if every leader is imbued with a determination to close with the enemy he will be unconsciously assisting his neighbour also, for as a rule **the best method of supporting a neighbouring unit is to advance.**

7. The distances between the firing line and supports will be determined by the company commanders, or the officers commanding each portion of the supports, according to the ground ; they will seldom be the same in every company, and may vary during the course of an advance. If the ground is favourable supports should close up to the firing line under cover ; on open ground the distance between them should be such that the supports will not suffer heavy losses from fire directed at the leading line (*see* Sec. **118**). The aim of officers commanding supports must be so to handle their commands as to be able to reinforce the firing line with as little delay as possible when required. Care must be taken not to dissipate energy by reinforcing in driblets. Reinforcement should usually be by bodies not smaller than platoons. In the later stages of an attack it is essential that reinforcing lines should carry up extra ammunition for the men in front.

8. Throughout the action the company commander will maintain communication with his platoon commanders, with the battalion commander, and with the companies on his flanks. He will as a rule accompany the final reinforcement of his company into the firing line.

9. As soon as he has received his orders the platoon commander should explain the situation to his subordinates and point out the line of advance. He must ensure that the movements of his platoon do not mask the fire of units on his flanks, and must endeavour to co-operate with neigh-

bouring units throughout the attack. He must direct the
fire of his platoon as long as it is possible for him to do so,
regulate the expenditure of ammunition, and take steps to
secure a further supply when required. He must watch the
enemy's movements and report at once to the company
commander and to neighbouring units if anything of importance is observed ; he must also be on the look-out for
signals from his company commander and should detail an
observer to assist him in this duty. During the advance
he must take every opportunity of rallying his command
on suitable ground. When the whole platoon is advancing
by rushes he must select and point out successive halting
places, and must himself lead the rush. After a successful
assault he must get the men in his vicinity under control
as quickly as possible in preparation for an immediate pursuit.

10. The duty of the section commander is to lead his section.
He must see that the direction is maintained, and that he
does not mask the fire of neighbouring sections. When the
advance is being made by sections, he must select and point
out the successive halting places of his section and must
regulate the number of men to occupy particular portions of
cover. He must control, and when necessary direct the fire
of his section (see Sec. 116), and, as reinforcements come up
into the firing line, must take all leaderless men in his neighbourhood under his command, giving them the range and
indicating targets. He must pass on quickly all reports
that come to him, and inform his platoon commander of any
hostile movements which he may observe.

11. All commanders should bear in mind that units are particularly liable to lose direction when moving forward from a
hedge or similar feature which lies obliquely to their line of
advance.

12. Combined action is always more likely to be successful than isolated effort, and so long as control is possible the individual man must watch his leader and do his best to carry out his intentions. When, however, the section is under heavy fire, section commanders cannot always exercise direct control, and in these circumstances men should endeavour to work in pairs, estimating the range for themselves, firing steadily, and husbanding their ammunition. If incapacitated from advancing, the soldier's first duty is to place his ammunition in a conspicuous place, ready to be picked up by other men, and all ranks must seize opportunities that offer for replenishing their ammunition in this manner.

13. If, when reinforcing the firing line, or at any other time, a soldier loses touch with his section commander, it is his duty to place himself under the orders of the nearest officer or non-commissioned officer, irrespective of the company or battalion to which he may belong.

14. No man is permitted to leave his platoon in action to take wounded to the rear, or for any other purpose, without special orders. After an action any unwounded man who has become separated from his company must rejoin it with the least possible delay.

124. *The assault and pursuit.*

1. The fact that superiority of fire has been obtained will usually be first observed from the firing line ; it will be known by the weakening of the enemy's fire, and perhaps by the movements of individuals or groups of men from the enemy's position towards the rear. The impulse for the assault must therefore often come from the firing line, and it is the duty of any commander in the firing line, who

sees that the moment for the assault has arrived, to carry it out, and for all other commanders to co-operate.

2. On rarer occasions the commander of the attacking force may be in a position to decide that the time has come to force a decision, and may throw in reinforcements from the rear so that the firing line may gain the necessary impulse for the assault. This will be more likely to occur when the enemy is strong and determined, and the fire fight at close infantry range has been prolonged and severe. In order to ensure an effective and concerted blow it is important that these reinforcements should be brought up well under control, that they should be in sufficient strength to create the necessary impulse, and that all ranks should understand exactly what is required of them.

3. Subordinate commanders in the firing line will decide when bayonets are to be fixed, in accordance with the local conditions of the combat and the nature of the ground. The commander who decides to assault will order the *charge* to be sounded, the call will at once be taken up by all buglers, and all neighbouring units will join in the charge as quickly as possible. During the delivery of the assault the men will cheer, bugles be sounded, and pipes played.

The bursts of artillery fire will have become frequent and intense at this period, the object of the artillery being to demoralize the defenders and reduce their volume of fire. Whether the artillery can continue firing until the assaulting infantry is actually on the point of closing with the enemy, or whether it should increase the range on the first sign of the assault must depend on the slope of the ground.

4. If the assault is successful, and the enemy driven from his position, immediate steps must be taken to get the attacking infantry in hand for the further work that lies before them.

The victory is as yet but half won ; decisive success will be achieved only by the annihilation of the enemy. A portion of the troops must at once be pushed forward to harry the retreating forces while the remainder are being re-formed, under their own officers if possible, in preparation for a relentless pursuit.

5. Owing to the possibility of hostile gun-fire being brought to bear on the captured position, units should not be re-formed on the position itself, but should move forward to the least exposed localities available. The task of re-forming units will usually fall to subordinate leaders.

6. Steps must be taken to meet a possible counter-attack.

7. As soon as re-formed, units must be ready to carry on the pursuit by day and night without regard to their exhaustion. To sustain a relentless pursuit the utmost energies of every commander must be exerted ; only indomitable will can overcome fatigue and carry the men forward. A commander must demand the impossible and not think of sparing his men. Those who fall out must be left behind and must no more stop the pursuit than casualties stopped the assault.

8. Infantry in pursuit should act with the greatest boldness and be prepared to accept risks. Delay for the purpose of detailed reconnaissance or for turning movements is not warranted, and the enemy must be attacked directly he is seen.

CHAPTER XI.

INFANTRY IN DEFENCE.

125. *Definition of the term defence.*

1. The term defence is used here in its broadest sense, and includes :—

    i. Active defence, in which the ultimate object in view is to create and seize a favourable opportunity for a decisive offensive.

    ii. Passive defence, in which the object may be to beat off an attack without hope of being able to turn the tables on the enemy by assuming the offensive at some stage of the fight, as, for example, in the defence of a fortified post weakly garrisoned.

    iii. The delaying action by means of manœuvre, in which efforts are directed to gaining time without risking defeat, as in the conduct of rearguards, or when awaiting the arrival of reinforcements.

THE ACTIVE DEFENCE.

126. *General principles.*

1. The troops will be divided into two main portions, one, known as the general reserve, to be held in readiness for the initiation of a general offensive when a favourable opportunity has been created, the other to create the desired opportunity by temporarily taking up a defensive position, and then to co-operate actively with the general reserve in its attack on the enemy.

2. In forming his plan of battle the commander has to determine the relative strength of these two parts, the time and place for the assumption of the offensive by the general reserve, and the general distribution, and methods of action of the remainder of the force. These will all vary with the commander's intentions and will largely depend upon the nature of the ground. On occasion his plan may be to strike the enemy directly the latter has committed his forces to the attack, and thus lost his power of manœuvre. In such a case it is not likely that a severe strain will be imposed upon the part of the force intended to create the opportunity for attack, which may therefore be comparatively weak or may even attain its object by manœuvring rather than by continuing to hold a definite position. At other times the commander may consider that his best chance of victory lies in allowing the enemy to exhaust his strength in endeavouring to capture a strong position before the offensive is assumed. In these circumstances it is necessary that both the position and the force allotted to hold it should be strong enough for the object in view.

3. Whatever may be the strategical situation, the underlying principles of defensive action which aims at decisive results are constant. **No natural or artificial strength of position will of itself compensate for loss of initiative when an enemy has time and liberty to manœuvre. The choice of a position and its preparation must therefore be made with a view to economizing the power expended on defence in order that the power of offence may be increased.**

4. Every position should be strengthened as far as time admits, with the object of reducing the number

of men required to hold it, and of thereby adding to the strength of the general reserve.

5. When it is possible to foresee a considerable time ahead that a suitable position exists which the enemy will be compelled to attack before he can advance further, elaborate preparations may be made for its defence. When, on the other hand, it is necessary to await the development of the enemy's plans before a suitable position can be selected, or when it is a question of the possibility of drawing him in a desired direction, it will be necessary to trust rather to a detailed reconnaissance of a considerable area of ground, and to arrange various alternative distributions of the force to meet the different courses of action open to the enemy.

127. *The choice of a defensive position.*

1. When the commander of a force has selected approximately the position to be defended, the next step is to decide on the line to be held and on the extent of front to be occupied. The object must be to obtain the maximum of fire effect on all ground over which the enemy can advance, with the minimum of exposure to his fire. An extensive field of fire from the position offers many advantages, but if the enemy be very superior in artillery a restricted field of fire combined with comparative security from his guns may give better results. It is difficult for attacking infantry to push home an assault against determined troops well protected from artillery fire even if the defenders have only a field of fire a few hundred yards in depth.

2. The extent of the front of the position must be proportionate to the object in view (*i.e.*, to the plan of battle) and to the force available.

If the frontage occupied in battle is so great as to roduce the force kept in hand for the ultimate initiation of the offensive much below half the total force available, the position may be considered too extended to be held with a view to decisive action.   `

On the other hand, too narrow a front may enable the enemy to develop early in the engagement strong flank attacks, which may make the position untenable before the time is ripe for the assumption of the offensive.

The flanks are always the weakest part of a position if they are open to attack, and an extension of front which, under other conditions, would be excessive, may be advisable if it enables one or both flanks to be posted strongly.   If the flanks can be made sufficiently strong the enemy may be forced to attempt to drive his assault home against the front of the position.   It is a great advantage if one flank, at least, can be posted so strongly as to compel the enemy to make his main efforts against the other, as this will usually enable the defender to foresee the probable direction of the enemy's main attack and to make his dispositions accordingly.

3. Behind the firing line it is important to have sufficient depth for manœuvre.   There should be good cover for supports and local reserves, and the nature of the ground should permit of these being moved either to the front or to a flank as may be required.

4. A position fulfilling all requirements can seldom, if ever, be found.   It will always be necessary in selecting one to balance various advantages and disadvantages.   But since, in active defence, the position is held only as a means of creating a favourable opportunity for eventual offensive, it is essential that the position should be chosen with a view to facilities for launching the attack.

Unless there be favourable ground for this, the position cannot be considered a suitable one for the object in view.

128. *The distribution of the troops detailed to defend the position.*

1. When a position is extensive it should be divided into sections, each of which should be assigned to a distinct unit. The extent of a section depends on the power of control of one commander, and must therefore vary according to the nature of the ground. It will be rare, however, even in the case of large forces, for the infantry garrison of a section to be more than a brigade.

2. The troops allotted to the defence of each section* of the position will be divided, as in the attack, into (i) firing line and, if necessary, supports, and (ii) local reserves.

3. The factors which affect the extent of frontage which may be held by the troops allotted to the defence of each section of the position are as varied as those which affect the question of frontage in attack. Even when the utmost development of rifle fire is required, not more than one man per yard can usefully be employed in one line. The number of men detailed for the firing line and supports of any section should therefore rarely exceed the number of yards in the total frontage of the section. When the ground is naturally very favourable to defence or can be made so artificially a less dense line should be sufficient, and not a man more than necessary should be used for this purpose. The strength

---

* The case considered here is that of a position divided into sections. When a position is not so divided, the action of the officer responsible for the defence of the whole position will be similar to the action of a commander of a section of the defence herein described.

of the local reserves may be estimated roughly at about that
of the firing line and supports, but must depend on the facilities
for defence and offence offered by the ground, and upon
the extent to which it has been possible to strengthen the
position.

4. The commander of each section will detail the number
of men required for the occupation of localities or portions of
the front, and will keep the remainder of the troops allotted
to him under his own orders as a local reserve.

5. The units allotted to the defence of localities or of
portions of the front, will find the firing line and supports.
But although the provision and action of local reserves are
the special business of commanders of sections of the defence,
commanders of battalions included in such sections may also
hold small local reserves in their own hands and undertake
minor local counter-attacks with them when the conditions
appear to be favourable for such action.   For instance,
portions of a position where the conditions are unfavourable
to a direct defence, may sometimes be better defended by
means of local reserves than by strengthening the firing line.

6. **Local reserves should not be employed to reinforce the firing line ;** every man in the firing line should
be made to understand that assistance will be given if required
in the form of a local counter-attack (*see* Sec. **131**, 3).

129. *The preparation of the position for defence.*

1. Defensive positions will usually include a number of
localities of special tactical importance.   The efforts of the
defender will be directed in the first instance to occupying
and securing these points, so that they may form pivots
upon which to hinge the defence of the remainder of the

position. The defences of these localities should be arranged so that they may give each other mutual support, and should always be allotted to a definite unit.

If these points are naturally strong or can be made so artificially, and if they are adequately garrisoned, so as to form a framework against which the enemy must expend his strength, the intervening ground need not be held in a continuous line. The object should rather be to utilise this intervening ground for local counter-attacks, while arranging for either direct or flanking fire, or both, within such ranges as may be decided on, to be brought to bear on all ground over which the enemy may advance.

A defensive position prepared in this manner lends itself to local counter-attacks, which keep alive an offensive spirit in the defenders, exhaust the enemy's powers, draw in his reserves, and thus prepare the way for the assumption of the offensive.

2. Where a defensive position is to be held at night or during fog, it will usually be necessary to supplement the system of occupying localities, described above, by a more continuous line of defence in order to prevent the enemy from penetrating the position. When a battle begun in daylight is not decided at dusk, it may be justifiable to employ local reserves to occupy the gaps in a defensive line. In any case the dispositions suitable for day will rarely be equally suitable for night, and it may be necessary to rearrange the defence.

3. The methods of preparing and entrenching localities and the various types of trenches are described in the Manual of Field Engineering. The preliminary measures should be based upon as thorough a reconnaissance as is possible by each commander of the area for which he is responsible.

The first step in the work of preparation is to improve the

field of fire, both by clearing the foreground and by taking ranges to all prominent objects. These ranges may be supplemented by fixing range marks, with which, as well as with the ranges taken, the troops should be made familiar.

Range cards (Plate XVII) will be found useful by infantry when occupying posts or positions of any kind, including outpost positions; they should be handed over to relieving units. Objects in or near the position, which might assist the enemy in ascertaining the range, should be removed if possible.

4. The chief point to keep in view in providing cover is that the fire from it should be effective, but facilities for concealment, control, communication, and for the supply of ammunition, food, and water must also be considered.

The concealment of trenches usually requires special measures. They should not be sited in exposed positions, such as the tops of bare hills or of prominent salients, if this can be avoided, and all excavations should be made to assimilate the background. Salients and advanced posts which are held in order to deny ground to the enemy, and not merely as a screen to the main position, are a weakness if they are exposed to artillery fire which cannot be answered, and if they cannot be supported by effective infantry fire. As a general rule it is better to leave such positions unoccupied, and for the ground between them and the main position to be defended by fire from the main position. On the other hand, advanced posts which can be supported effectively by fire from the main position are often of value in breaking up an attack.

Generally speaking, it is easier to arrange covered communication with high-sited trenches, but these often entail a certain amount of dead ground in front of the position.

It is sometimes possible to avoid this by arranging for the fire from one trench to sweep the ground in front of another and *vice versa*, but too much reliance should not be placed on this method as it is difficult for the garrison of a trench which is being heavily attacked to fire in any other direction than that of its immediate opponents. Trenches placed at the foot of slopes are more easily concealed and admit of a more grazing fire than high-sited trenches. They are therefore usually preferable, even though the supply of reinforcements, ammunition, food, and water to their garrison may involve difficulties. Trenches which can bring fire to bear at close range on to the ground over which the attack must pass, and which are themselves concealed from the attackers in the early stages, are most valuable in surprising the enemy at critical periods.

5. The general position and extent of obstacles will be decided by the commander of each section. who in fixing their position and nature must bear in mind the need for facilities for local counter-attack and for the eventual assumption of the offensive.

6. Deep trenches in covered positions in rear of the fire trenches may be usefully provided for that part of the firing line which it is decided to hold in support, or for the whole garrison of the advanced trenches till it is required. When garrisons are thus held back, a few men must be posted in the trenches to keep a look out, and communicating trenches will usually be a necessary addition, in order to ensure covered connection with the fire trenches. If it is not possible to provide cover and communications for the supports, the latter may be merged in the firing line from the outset.

Local reserves should be posted under natural cover if available, and their rapid movement in any direction in which they may be required must be facilitated. If it is necessary to make artificial cover for reserves it must be made clear that this is not a secondary position, but that the cover is merely prepared to shelter the troops until they are required.

7. Buildings, villages, and woods are particular forms of the defensive localities referred to in paragraph 1 of this section. The commander of the section in which they are will normally decide whether they are to be occupied or not. Buildings, when naturally strong or properly prepared are of great value in the defence, but they may form an easy target if exposed to artillery fire. Usually, therefore, they should not be actually held, except by look-out men, when under artillery fire, but should be prepared for occupation when the enemy's artillery fire ceases, and garrisons should be held ready for the purpose. (*See also* Chapter XIII.)

130. *Use of covering troops.*

1. The skilful use of covering troops will often assist the defender in concealing his dispositions and in surprising the enemy.

2. The cavalry, **supported by the other arms when necessary,** may do much to screen the main position, to mislead the hostile commander as to its exact situation and extent, to induce him to deploy prematurely, and to fatigue his troops in groping for skilfully covered flanks, while his uncertainty will be prolonged if the troops occupying the main position are carefully concealed and withhold their fire until the last possible moment.

3. Covering troops employed in this way should be withdrawn in time to prevent them from becoming closely engaged

and from masking the fire from the main position. The commander of the covering troops should be given clear instructions on these points. The decision to employ covering troops rests normally with the commander of the force, but commanders of sections are at liberty to deal with special features, such as woods and villages (*see* Chapter XIII), in front of their positions, by pushing forward detachments to break up the enemy's advance, to command otherwise dead ground, to induce a premature deployment, or to create opportunities for local counter-attacks. The objection to the use of such localities for this purpose is the difficulty of choosing the right moment for withdrawal. If the garrison withdraws too soon only half its work will be completed ; if too late it may not be able to make good its retirement, and other troops sent to its assistance may be involved in action in disadvantageous circumstances.

131. *The conduct of the infantry fight in the defence of a position.*

1. A favourable opportunity for assuming the offensive may occur early or may be long deferred. In either case the chance of success depends largely on the troops allotted to the position holding it against all attacks, without calling for reinforcements.

2. The duty of the firing line is to prevent the enemy from advancing on to the position and to exhaust him by an obstinate and determined defence of the ground allotted to it, thus preparing for the ultimate offensive. The general principles governing the use and control of fire in the defence have been described in Secs. **116** and **117.**

Subordinate commanders with the firing line will decide

when bayonets are to be fixed, in accordance with the local conditions of the combat and the nature of the ground, but this should be done before the enemy reaches a position from which it is possible to carry out the assault.

Any part of the firing line kept back in support will be used to replace casualties in the front line and to infuse fresh vigour into the defence.

3. The enemy will not ordinarily make a serious attempt to drive his attack home at all points, and it is important to discover, as soon as possible, where he intends to apply his main strength. Before either side can deliver a decisive attack it is to be expected that there will be a prolonged fight for fire superiority. During this struggle the object to be aimed at is not merely to wear down the enemy's firing line until it is incapable of further advance, but **to drive it back so that the enemy may be forced to use up his local reserves to restore the battle. This can be done by means of vigorous local counter-attacks, delivered whenever a suitable opportunity occurs.** Such opportunities will arise when the enemy's firing line comes within reach without sufficient support, and when fire superiority, even though only temporary, has been gained.

Local counter-attacks may be initiated by any commander who keeps local reserves in his hands, but the most important will be those carried out by the reserves of sections under the direction of the commanders of sections of the defence.

To achieve its purpose a local counter-attack should compel the enemy to expend more force than is involved in its delivery. Counter-attacks against strong tactical points are, therefore, usually inadvisable, and for the same reason success should not be followed up too far.

Officers in command of local reserves should previously reconnoitre the ground over which they may have to lead a counter-attack, and must, by carefully watching the progress of the fight, and by arranging beforehand for the co-operation of other units, including artillery, be ready for instant action when a favourable opportunity occurs. The danger to be guarded against is that troops may go too far and get out of hand. Before starting, therefore, commanders of local reserves must decide the approximate distance that the attack is to go, and must see that this is understood by all ranks. They must also consider beforehand the means of covering their subsequent withdrawal, and it will sometimes be advisable to keep back a small portion of their force for this purpose.

4. In a bayonet fight the impetus of a charging line gives it moral and physical advantages over a stationary line. Infantry on the defensive should therefore always be ready to meet a bayonet charge by a counter-charge. This counter-charge, however, should not be made prematurely. The enemy cannot fire effectively while charging, and can rarely be well supported by covering fire. He thus offers at such a time a very vulnerable target, of which advantage should be taken so long as a steady and well directed fire can be brought to bear on him. Should, however, the volume of fire be insufficient to check the assailant, a **counter-charge must be made before he has actually reached the position**. When it is made success will fall to the line which is best in hand and charges with most spirit and determination.

132. *The battalion in the active defence.*

1. The battalion commander, in arranging for the defence
of a portion of a position, will be guided by the principles
given in the preceding sections.   When acting with other
battalions in the defence of a section, it will depend upon
local conditions whether he keeps a local reserve in his
hands or not (*see* Sec. **128**, 5).   His method of issuing orders
will be similar to that described for the attack.

2. If acting alone, his chief object will be to defend the
position with the fewest possible numbers in order to have in
his hands as strong as possible a force with which to assume
the offensive.

3. The duties of company, platoon, and section commanders
are generally similar to their duties in the attack (*see* Sec. **123**).

Care must be taken that the trenches are concealed from the
enemy, that ranges are taken and communicated to the men,
that ample ammunition and water is available, and that look-
out men are posted to watch the front before the enemy
approaches and during pauses in the attack.

133. *The assumption of the offensive.*

1. A commander who decides upon an active defence,
changes from the defensive to the offensive by launching
his general reserve.

The considerations which affect the size, composition,
and position of this force and the questions of the choice
of the time for launching the attack, and of the direction
which it should take, are dealt with in Field Service Regulations Part, I.

2. The methods of the general reserve when assuming the

offensive from the defensive are generally similar to those described in Sec. **121.**   But since the object in view is to take advantage of a favourable opportunity, which will usually be fleeting, many of the preliminary measures, which are desirable before a more deliberate attack is launched, must be dispensed with. (*See* Sec. **122, 4.**)   The action of the infantry must therefore be most vigorous and the firing line must from the outset be as strong as possible.

3. There will probably be little time for issuing detailed orders, but the direction and manner of carrying out the attack should be carefully pointed out to all subordinate commanders, who will explain the same to the troops, and impress on them the importance of getting to close quarters quickly.

4. In order that no time may be lost when the moment for action arrives, commanders of troops allotted to the general reserve should take every opportunity beforehand of reconnoitring ground over which they may have to act and of explaining the situation to their subordinates.

5. The assumption of the offensive should not be confined to the advance of the general reserve alone.   Commanders of sections of the defence who are permitted by the local situation to do so must at once join actively in the attack unless express orders to the contrary have been received, and any decisive success which the movement obtains must be the signal for the whole force to press the enemy with the utmost vigour.

THE PASSIVE DEFENCE.

134. *General principles.*

1. A passive defence (*see* Sec. **125**) can, at most, repulse an

enemy's attack ; it can never, of itself, achieve a decisive success. When employed against an active enemy, who has liberty of manœuvre, it is exposed to the risk of crushing defeat. For these reasons resort should never be had to a passive defence when the end in view can be obtained by other means.

2. When the object in view is merely to gain time it is usually preferable to employ manœuvre rather than passive defence (*see* Sec. **135**). Passive defence may, however, be used with advantage to gain time when the enemy's power of manœuvre is limited, as, for example, when a position which it is difficult to turn can be occupied.

3. The general principles of the defence of such a position are similar to those described in Secs. **128** and **129** in the case of active defence, with the exception that, as no general reserve is required to initiate a general offensive, almost the whole of the troops may be utilised for the defence of the position. The frontage occupied may therefore be greater than would otherwise be the case, and it will be an advantage if both the front and flanks of the position are covered by obstacles. Fire may be opened at long range ; and every effort should be made to impose upon the enemy and delay his attack. (*See* Sec. **130**.)

4. The garrison of a defensive post, which is not strong enough to resort to an active defence, may have to confine its efforts to beating off attack, that is to say, to a passive defence. Instructions for the organization and preparation of defensive posts are contained in the Manual of Field Engineering.

THE DELAYING ACTION BY MEANS OF MANŒUVRE.

135. *General principles.*

1. The conditions under which a commander may seek to delay an enemy by manœuvre and the various methods he may adopt are described in Field Service Regulations, Part 1.

The methods to be employed by infantry will depend chiefly upon the decision of the commander based on these considerations.

2. Delaying action by means of manœuvre demands of infantry great mobility, endurance, and the power of rapid marching. It, therefore, calls for a high degree of training and discipline.

CHAPTER XII.

THE ENCOUNTER BATTLE—RETIREMENTS.

136. *The Encounter Battle.*

1. There will be many occasions when both forces are advancing to attack and when the opposing advanced guards will meet while their respective main bodies are still in march formation. On such occasions the commander whose force is best in hand, and can deploy first, will reap far-reaching advantages. In place of the difficulty of approaching an enemy in position, he may now be able to attack his opponent's main forces while still extricating themselves from march formations and quite unready for battle. Rapidity of action is therefore of supreme importance, and at no time is the initiative of subordinate commanders, based on a knowledge of their commander's intentions and an intelligent anticipation of his plans, more required.

The value of early successes, however small, can hardly be over-estimated, for they will usually cause the enemy to hesitate and force him to conform.

2. In the circumstances of an encounter battle it is

generally necessary to dispense in the early stages with the
more deliberate preparations for launching infantry to the
attack which have been described in the previous sections.
A detailed reconnaissance and a formal issue of orders will
rarely be possible. It is therefore more than ever important
that all infantry commanders should keep themselves informed
of the action of the neighbouring units by detaching officers
to report the progress of the latter, or by other means, and
that they should report their own action and the development of the situation frequently and promptly.

3. As the battle develops more deliberate methods may
become possible and pauses in the advance may be unavoidable. These pauses should be used to supplement such
preliminary reconnaissances as it has been possible to carry
out, to confirm messages and verbal instructions by complete written orders, and, when necessary, to reorganize
units.

4. Should the commander of the force, owing to the
general strategical situation, or for other reasons, be compelled to await attack with a view to assuming the offensive
later, it becomes the duty of the advanced troops to gain
time and space for him to make his dispositions. If the
enemy succeeds in deploying first there is a danger that
the advanced troops may be enveloped or defeated before
the remainder can reach the battlefield. The rôle of the
leading infantry in such cases is to delay the enemy and
hamper his deployment. Subsequently the action of the
infantry is similar to that of a force acting on the defensive with a view to the eventual assumption of the
offensive.

137. *Retirements.*

1. Retirements in face of the enemy must be conducted with the greatest circumspection. A hurried retreat is not only a fruitful source of panic but a great encouragement to the enemy. A steady deliberate retirement, on the other hand, carried out in silence and good order, imposes respect and caution on the hostile troops. The general principles governing the action of a rearguard to a retreating force are contained in Field Service Regulations, Part I.

2. In retiring under fire, portions of the firing line should usually retire alternatively, affording each other mutual support by taking up successive fire positions at some considerable distance apart, from which the retirement of the portion nearest the enemy can be covered.

3. Machine guns skilfully handled may be of great assistance in movements of this nature, and the detachments must, if necessary, be prepared to sacrifice themselves to cover the retirement of their infantry.

4. Men retiring under fire in extended order should, if well in hand, move from cover to cover at the quickest possible pace, a few men, preferably the most active, being left behind at each halt to cover the retirement of the remainder, and rapid fire being used to deceive the enemy as to the numbers left behind. If, however, the men are at all shaken, as when an attack has failed, every effort must be made to rally and restore order. All ranks should exert themselves to the utmost to ensure that the retirement is carried out, notwithstanding losses, with steadiness and precision.

5. If the enemy presses hard, a sudden counter-attack, not followed up too far, may give good results.

6. When mounted troops are available, they will be used to cover the final withdrawal of the infantry from each successive fire position.

CHAPTER XIII.

FIGHTING IN CLOSE COUNTRY, WOODS, AND VILLAGES.

138. *Influence of close country upon tactics.*

1. Any tract of country in which view and movement are seriously restricted by woods, fences, or high crops is " close country." In such areas the enclosures may be bounded in very different ways—for example, by simple wire fences which do not interfere with view, do not afford cover from fire, and are a considerable obstacle to movement ; by dense hedges, which give cover from view but not from fire, and are difficult to surmount ; or by high banks, which afford complete cover from view and fire, and are not a serious obstacle to infantry. The influence of enclosed country upon tactical methods also changes with the season of the year, and is not the same in winter when trees and hedges are bare as it is in summer when they are in full leaf.

2. Generally speaking, in close country, owing to the limitation of the field of view and of fire, the employment of artillery is restricted ; machine guns, on the other hand, are well adapted for supporting infantry closely. Close country favours delaying action, but not necessarily a protracted defence, for it is often possible for the attackers to work up to the defenders unseen. It hampers deployment both for attack and for counter-attack, and makes it more difficult to discover when and where to strike an effective

blow. An important characteristic of close country is loss of higher control, which calls for more initiative on the part of subordinates in order to ensure combination.

3. Troops fighting in close country are usually very sensitive as to their flanks, as they are unable to see what is going on. This fact affects the defence more than the attack, for there is danger that a defended line penetrated at one point may give way everywhere. Further it is particularly difficult in close country for the defenders to deliver local counter-attacks in the most effective direction, or to organize converging fire against captured localities.

139. *The attack in close country.*

1. Close country enables the attacker to approach his enemy with less loss than is usually experienced in more open ground, gives him facilities for screening his movements, and allows him favourable opportunities for surprising his opponent. To reap these advantages the attacker must be accustomed to manœuvre in close country, and must realise and make careful preparation to overcome the difficulties likely to be met. A thorough reconnaissance is of more than usual importance.

2. Troops detailed for attack should not be prematurely deployed. In close country affording cover from view the advance may be safely carried out in close formation provided the service of protection is properly performed.

3. It is rarely possible in close country to keep the objective in constant view. Special care is therefore necessary if the direction of the attack is to be preserved. Even when the objective is clearly visible at the beginning of an attack it is advisable to take precautions in case it may

disappear from view. The desire to make the best use of
cover or to pass an obstacle at the easiest place frequently
causes infantry to lose direction. The simplest method of
maintaining direction is by guides or in default of guides by
compass. Before infantry advances to the attack in close
country the bearing of the objective should be made known
to all officers and non-commissioned officers in possession of
compasses.

4. Owing to the short range to which the firing line may
be able to approach before fire is opened, it must be prepared
to meet with strong opposition directly its position is dis-
covered, and must itself be ready to develop a considerable
volume of fire at any moment.

5. It may at times be advisable to move supports and
reserves forward in file rather than in lines, taking advantage
of the concealment offered by hedges or banks for this purpose. It must be remembered, however, that hedges leading
in the direction of the enemy may become a dan₃erous trap
if enfiladed by hostile fire.

6. In country which is intersected by small woods, high
banks, and hedges, troops in one field are often ignorant of
what is happening to troops in adjoining fields. In these
circumstances co-operation is a matter of difficulty, and can
cnly be insured by careful preparation. The most effective
method of keeping touch when on the move is for the commander of troops in each field to detail men to follow along
the boundaries of that field with a view to reporting the
movements of neighbouring troops and the development
of the situation. These men may also be used as inter-
mediaries in passing orders and messages, when the ordinary
means of communication fail.

7. The reorganization of units is specially important in

close country. All commanders, however subordinate, must endeavour to minimize the difficulties of control by taking every opportunity to get men in hand.

140. *The defence in close country.*

1. The chief difficulties of a protracted defence in close country have been described in Sec. **138**. These difficulties may to some extent be removed by clearing the foreground and by improving communications.

2. Sufficient preparation to prevent the attacker from concealing the direction of his main attack more effectively than he could do in open country will however be rarely possible. It will be advantageous usually to throw forward a screen to force early deployment, this screen falling back gradually on to or round the main defensive position. This end can also be achieved by pushing forward small bodies of infantry along the roads open to the enemy. It will often be advisable to penetrate the enemy's screen by means of local counter-attacks in order to discover his plans and defeat the heads of his columns before they deploy. Such attacks, being specially intended to obtain information, may usually be delivered sooner than counter-attacks intended to repulse the enemy's firing line and to force him to use up his reserves (*see* Sec. **131**, 3.).

3. The difficulties of the defence depend very much on the nature of the country. When enclosed country is flat artillery has few opportunities, but when it is undulating, though the field of fire at close infantry ranges is often very limited, it is usually possible to make effective use of fire at longer distances. Enclosed country is also frequently provided with such a network of roads as to reduce considerably the difficulties of manœuvre.

4. As a general rule commanding positions in enclosed country, unless they have exceptional advantages in the form of an increased field of fire, should be avoided. They serve as an easy objective to the enemy's infantry and artillery and obviate many of the difficulties which the attacker has to overcome.

WOOD AND VILLAGE FIGHTING.

141. *General considerations.*

1. Woods and villages may be expected to exert a powerful influence over the movements of troops operating in their immediate neighbourhood. Not only are troops instinctively attracted towards them during an action, in search either of a covered approach or of some tangible object to attack or defend, but the fact of such places being named on a map increases the probability of fighting in their locality, in that they may be used to define the boundaries of sections of the attack or defence, or as points of direction for portions of the force. An added importance attaches to villages from the facilities they afford for obtaining water, supplies, and shelter.

2. In future wars it may be expected that woods will frequently be used to conceal movements from the observation of hostile aircraft, while in an extended battle front it may often occur that parts of the force will be compelled to operate in woods and villages even though the remainder are fighting in the open. Woods and villages may also be used in front of a defensive position to command otherwise dead ground, to induce a premature deployment, or to break up an enemy's attack (*see* Sec. **130**).

142. *General principles of wood fighting.*

1. The movements of large bodies of troops in a wood will be slow, and communications much hampered. Scouts must reconnoitre well ahead of the troops, and must advance by bounds in the usual manner. When collision with the enemy is expected, small parallel columns, in fours or file, at deploying interval, will usually be the most convenient formation for an advance, and in order to reduce the mingling of units when fighting begins, the distribution of companies should be in depth rather than in breadth. Careful arrangements must be made for preserving lateral touch, and for guarding the flanks. The maintenance of direction will often be difficult, and it will usually be necessary to march on a compass bearing, the same precautions being taken as for a night advance.

2. The action of artillery and of mounted troops will be greatly restricted, both in attack and defence, and infantry must largely depend on its own efforts to attain success.

3. Fighting will, as a rule, take place only at close range, and both in attack and defence infantry should be ready to develop a strong fire at the outset, and to charge with the bayonet at the first opportunity.

4. All commanders must keep small reserves in hand to meet counter attacks or unforeseen emergencies, and stragglers must be collected to form new reserves.

5. Higher control will be a matter of great difficulty, and much will depend on the maintenance of intercommunication and on the initiative and resource of subordinate leaders.

6. The curtailment of the danger zone will place the defence at an added disadvantage, but opportunities for surprise

and for misleading the attacking force will frequently present themselves. Opportunities for counter-attack will also frequently occur, but the difficulty of seeing what is happening in the immediate neighbourhood makes it of more than usual importance that counter-attacks should not be carried too far.

6. In wood fighting generally, infantry who use the bayonet have the best chance of success.

143. *Attack on a wood.*

1. The attack on a wood will consist of one or more of the following three phases, each of which will as a rule be entirely different in character, namely, the fight for the edge of the wood, the struggle in the interior, and the debouching from the wood on the enemy's side. In the first the attacker will probably have artillery predominance ; in the second the guns on both sides can do little to assist ; while in the third the defender will usually have superiority in artillery fire.

2. The attack on the edge of a wood differs in no way from the attack on any other position.

When once the edge has been gained, immediate steps must be taken to get the troops in hand, and to guard against a possible counter-attack. Small parties must at the same time be sent forward to reconnoitre the wood and gain touch with the retreating enemy. Rides and clearings, especially those which run diagonally in the direction of the enemy, must be examined with particular care before troops emerge on them, as the opposite sides or ends may be held by the enemy, and the attacking force subjected to a heavy frontal or enfilade fire.

3. Machine guns may be usefully employed in the firing line in the interior of a wood, and it may also be possible to bring up small portions of artillery in close support.

4. Particular care must be taken to guard against counter-attacks during the advance through a wood, and to protect the flanks. If the wood forms part of an enemy's defensive line, communication must be established with the attacking troops on both flanks, in order to prevent the troops inside the wood from debouching too soon.

5. When available, detachments of engineers should accompany troops advancing through woods, in order to assist in the demolition of obstacles.

6. If the enemy can open effective fire on the attackers as they issue from the wood, the outer edge of which may be prepared with abattis and entanglements, the advantage of covered approach will probably be overbalanced by the disadvantage of offering an easy target at a known range, and it may be better to seek another line of advance. If this is not possible, very careful arrangements must be made before attempting to debouch. Gaps must be made in any obstacles that have been prepared; the troops must be deployed some little distance inside the wood; arrangements must be made for the strongest possible artillery support; and, if possible, the advance of the infantry should be simultaneous with the advance of the attacking troops on either flank of the wood. When all is ready the infantry should press forward into the open in one rush until the danger zone at the edge of the wood is passed. On such occasions it will, in default of other cover, be better to halt in the open, well clear of the wood, than to pause in the neighbourhood of its edge.

144. A wood in the defence.

1. If a force is acting temporarily on the defensive, and the general line to be occupied includes a wood or woods, the question as to whether or not the line of defence should include the wood will depend on the configuration of the ground, the general disposition of the force, and the extent and nature of the wood itself.

2. Generally speaking, if the wood is of small extent and can **be outflanked, the most suitable position for the infantry will** be in front of it. If, on the other hand, the wood is large, and the configuration of the ground and general disposition of the force admit, it may be preferable to take up a position in rear, with the object of bringing a heavy artillery and infantry fire to bear on the enemy at close range when he attempts to emerge.

When it is desired to make use of a wood in front of a defensive position with a view to breaking up an enemy's attack it will usually be advantageous to hold the front of the wood.

3. In the case of a position being taken up in rear of a wood, it may sometimes be advisable to throw detachments forward into the wood itself with a view to harassing the enemy's advance, or if suitable clearings exist, to offer a stubborn resistance at such points. If time permits it may, in the absence of suitable clearings, even be advisable to clear portions of the wood for this purpose. Abattis and entanglements should be prepared both inside the wood and at its edge, and careful arrangements made for the withdrawal of the advanced troops well ahead of the enemy.

4. In holding the front face of a wood, though the wood itself may provide valuable cover for supports and reserves, it is rarely advisable to hold its actual edge, which usually

presents an easy target to the enemy's artillery. If is often possible by clearing undergrowth and the lower branches of trees to establish a firing line some distance inside the wood, or trenches may be sited well in front of it, covered communication with the supports or reserves inside being arranged.

When the front edge of a wood is held, and guns are used in close support, careful arrangements must be made beforehand for their rapid withdrawal to the rear in the case of necessity.

Should the enemy succeed in entering the wood, counter-attacks must at once be delivered on the initiative of subordinate commanders, and every effort made to dislodge him at the point of the bayonet.

5. When it is for any reason desired to act on the defensive in a large wood, and the outer line is too extensive to be held by the troops available, the wood may be defended effectively from a position prepared in the interior. A short field of fire will then be sufficient to prevent the attacker, who cannot easily be supported by artillery fire from leaving cover to continue his advance.

A position of this nature should be on some well-defined feature, such as a road, a ride, or stream. It should be artificially strengthened by means of breastworks, abattis, &c., and the ground in front should be cleared as far as time permits. Guns and machine guns should be placed in position with the infantry, special arrangements being made for their prompt withdrawal in case of necessity.

145. *Attack on a village.*

1. It may be presumed that an enemy defending a village, whether in front of or forming part of his defensive line,

will usually have prepared infantry trenches in front and to the flanks of the village itself. The conduct of the attack will in its initial stages, therefore, be similar to the attack of any other prepared position.

2. When, however, a village is obstinately defended by the enemy, it may sometimes be advisable, during the later stages of an attack, to mask the village with the troops on its front while neighbouring units press forward on both flanks, rather than to attempt its capture by assault.

3. When the capture of a village is necessary before the units on either flank can advance, recourse to street or house-to-house fighting will sometimes be unavoidable. As soon as a footing has been gained on the outskirts of the village, the troops must be reorganized in preparation for a further advance, which should be directed simultaneously on to as many points as possible. The probability of vigorous counter-attacks at this period must not be overlooked. When once the interior of the village has been gained, the struggle will resolve itself into the individual efforts of groups of men ; higher control will often be impossible, and subordinate leaders will influence the fight chiefly by their personal example. Every effort should, however, be made to maintain intercommunication, and this can usually be best achieved by sending back information to some pre-arranged point in rear.

4. All points gained, such as cross roads or important buildings, should at once be strengthened, so that attempts to recapture them may be defeated, and that they may serve as supporting points to a further advance.

5. When once the attacking troops have entered the village, their supporting artillery can be of little assistance, but it may be possible to bring single guns forward to destroy barri-

cades, and generally to assist the advance. Machine guns will also be of great assistance at this time.

6. When the attacking troops are about to emerge from the cover of a village, the same precautions must be taken as described in Sec. **143**, 6, the supporting guns covering the advance by engaging the hostile artillery.

146. *Defence of a village.*

1. When a village forms part of a general defensive line, the considerations which affect the question of its defence will be similar to those discussed in Sec. **144**, but the facilities it affords for water, cover, and shelter may usually be expected to point to the advisability of its inclusion in the main position.

2. In arranging for the defence of a village, whether it be isolated or in the main position, a definite garrison should always be allotted to it, and the defence of the whole village placed in the hands of one commander. The commander will divide the village into sub-commands as required, and will keep a reserve under his own hand.

3. It will usually be advisable to arrange for the garrison to be located, during the earlier stages of an attack, in trenches well to the front or on the flanks rather than in the actual buildings, which may be an easy mark for hostile artillery. If the configuration of the ground will admit, these trenches should be so arranged that a flanking fire can be brought to bear on the attacking troops as they approach, and guns may sometimes be posted in close support of the infantry, careful arrangements being made for their withdrawal, in case of necessity.

4. In preparing the interior of a village for defence houses should be loop-holed, communications from house to house

improved or improvised where required, and roads barricaded with a view to offering a stubborn resistance at close quarters (*see also* Manual of Field Engineering, Chapter VII).   Special preparations should be made at important points such as cross roads, village greens, or market squares, trenches and breastworks being arranged on the defender's side of these places, and it may sometimes be advisable to prepare a central " keep."   Communication with the commander of the village and the various portions of the garrison will usually be best achieved by sending back messages to some central point in rear.

5. Should the enemy succeed in entering the village, every effort must be made to dislodge him by means of counter-attacks delivered on the initiative of commanders of sub-sections of the defence.   The flanks will be specially liable to attack at this time and special precautions must be taken for their protection.

6. In the event of the defenders being forced back to their positions in the interior the retirement should be covered by vigorous bayonet charges and by fire from the houses.   Every effort must be made to keep the men in hand, and subordinate leaders must realise that their personal bearing at this time will have the greatest influence on the fight.

7. In instructing troops in the principles of street fighting, the comparative difficulties of shooting to the right or left from a window should be explained, together with the corollary as to which is the safer side of a street to remain on when advancing in face of the enemy.

CHAPTER XIV.

OUTPOSTS.

147. *General principles.*

1. Every body of troops when halted will be protected by outposts.

2. The duty of outposts is to give warning of any threatened attack, and in the event of attack to gain time, at any sacrifice, for the commander of the force protected to put his plan of action into execution. A force can only be regarded as secure from surprise when every body of the enemy within striking distance is so closely watched that it can make no movement without its immediately becoming known to the outposts.

The first duty of outposts, therefore, is observation of the enemy, the second duty resistance.

3. *Observation of the enemy* will consist of—

   i. Keeping such a close watch on all bodies of the enemy within reach of the outposts that no movement can be made unobserved.

   ii. Watching all approaches along which an enemy might advance.

   iii. Examining all neighbouring localities in which his patrols might be concealed, or which he might occupy preparatory to an attack.

Resistance will consist of delaying the enemy on a prepared defensive line, called the outpost line of resistance, until further orders are received from the commander of the protected force.

4. Outpost troops will usually consist of cavalry or cyclists and infantry working in co-operation. The mounted troops will be responsible for the duties of observation at a distance from the outpost line; the infantry for resistance and for their own immediate protection against surprise.

The outpost mounted troops will carry out their duty by means of patrols pushed well forward in the direction of the enemy. The outpost infantry will be divided into piquets and supports, the former to furnish sentry groups and to hold the outpost line of resistance, the latter to reinforce the piquets when required. Outpost infantry may also be required to furnish patrols (*see* Sec. **156**) and on occasions a portion of it may be held back to form an outpost reserve (*see* Sec. **149**).

5. Outpost work is most exhausting; not a man nor a horse more than absolutely necessary must be employed. The duty of observation must never be relaxed, whatever the distance of the enemy, but the number of troops detailed for resistance will depend on the ground, the distance of the enemy, and the tactical situation.

6. When there is any chance of a force coming in conflict with the enemy, the commander, when halting, should first decide on his dispositions in case of attack, and then arrange the quartering of his command and the general position of the outposts accordingly.

7. The distance of the outpost position from the troops protected is regulated by the time which the latter will require to prepare for action, and by the importance of preventing

the enemy's artillery from approaching within effective
artillery range of the ground on which these troops will
deploy if attacked. On the other hand, especially in the case
of small forces, the distance must not be such as would
permit of the outposts being cut off, or as would necessitate
the employment of an undue proportion of men on outpost
duty.

8. In the case of a force spread over a considerable frontage,
or one distributed in depth, the commander will usually divide
the outpost line decided on into sections, delegating responsibility for the holding of each section to the commander of
a subordinate unit or formation, and defining the limits of
sections by distinctive features, such as trees, cottages, or
streams. A road is not a suitable boundary for a section.
Each subordinate commander concerned will then detail
the necessary troops for his own portion of the outpost line
and will appoint an officer to command them.* He will
also be responsible that his outpost arrangements are co-
ordinated with those of the sections on his flanks.

9. In the case of a small force the commander will usually
himself detail the whole of the outpost troops and appoint
an officer to command them.*

10. It will sometimes be advisable that the advanced,
flank, and rear guards which have protected the force on
the march should be ordered to find the outposts.

11. When outpost troops are detailed from the main body
the troops which have covered the march will remain responsible for protection until relieved by the outposts. When
the march is resumed outposts must not be withdrawn till

---

* This officer will be designated the outpost commander.

the troops responsible for the protection of the march are in position.

12. To see without being seen is one of the first principles of outpost duty. All troops on outpost must therefore be carefully concealed.

13. Machine-guns with outposts may be employed to sweep approaches and to cover ground which an enemy in advancing may be compelled to pass or to occupy.

14. Detachments in close proximity to the enemy must avoid useless collisions. Attempts to carry off detached posts, sentries, &c., unless with some special object, are to be avoided, as they serve no good end, give rise to reprisals, and tend to disturb the main body.

15. The outposts will stand to arms one hour before it begins to get light and remain under arms until the patrols, which should be sent out at that time (*see* Sec. **156, 6**), report that there is no sign of an immediate attack. When the outposts are relieved in the morning, the relief should reach the outposts half an hour before it begins to get light. The troops relieved will not return to camp until the patrols report all clear.

16. No compliments will be paid when on outpost duty.

148. *Duties of an outpost commander.*

1. An outpost commander (*see* Sec. **147**, paras. 8 and 9) should be given information on the following points :—

  i. What is known of the enemy, and of other bodies of our own troops.

  ii. Intentions of the commander who appoints him, if the enemy attacks.

  iii. Where the force to be covered will halt.

iv. The general position to be occupied by the outpost troops under his command and, if there are other troops on his flanks, the limits of the line for which he is responsible.

v. Detail of the troops allotted to him.

vi. Hour at which they will be relieved.

vii. Where reports are to be sent.

2. After receiving the above information he will give such orders as are immediately necessary for protection against surprise. He will then allot tasks to his mounted troops and will decide on a line of resistance for the outpost infantry, dividing the frontage among the outpost companies at his disposal. When there are other outpost troops on his flanks, he will co-ordinate his arrangements with those of his neighbouring outpost commanders, and will ensure that no ground on his flanks remains unwatched.

3. In choosing an outpost line of resistance, he will remember that retirements of advanced troops on to a supporting line are always dangerous, particularly at night. As a general rule, therefore, the piquets should be posted on the line of resistance, which must be chosen with this object in view.

Co-operation, inter-communication, and the exercise of command will be facilitated by placing the piquets along well-defined natural features, or in the vicinity of roads; but this must not outweigh the necessity for the best tactical dispositions possible Commanding ground is not only unessential, but may sometimes be disadvantageous. At night little of the country in front can be seen from high ground, and rifle fire, except at close range, is useless. For night work, therefore, if the general configuration of the ground permits, it may be advisable to select a line along low ground for the outpost line of resistance, with a sky line in front which an approaching enemy would be obliged to cross.

4. The extent of frontage to be allotted to each company will depend on the probabilities of attack, the defensive capabilities of the outpost position, and, where they exist, on the number of approaches to be guarded. The limits of the frontage allotted to each company should be carefully defined, as in the case of sections of the outpost line (*see* Sec. 147, 8).

5. As soon as the foregoing details have been decided on, an outpost commander will issue orders on the following points :—

> i. Information of the enemy and our own troops so far as they affect the outposts.
>
> ii. General line to be occupied by the outposts ; frontage or number of roads allotted to each outpost company ; and situation of the reserve (*see* Sec. 149).
>
> iii. Disposition of outpost mounted troops.
>
> iv. Dispositions in case of attack. Generally the outpost line of resistance and degree of resistance to be offered.
>
> v. Special arrangements by night.
>
> vi. Smoking, lighting fires, and cooking.
>
> vii. The hour at which outposts will be relieved.
>
> viii. His own position.

6. If he finds it unnecessary to employ all the troops placed at his disposal, he will decide whether to retain the surplus as a reserve or to send them back to the main body (*see* Sec. 149).

7. As soon as the outposts are in position he will inform the commander who appointed him. He will also be responsible for maintaining communication with the main body.

149. *The reserve.*

1. The necessity, or otherwise, for the provision of a reserve depends on circumstances, such as the size of the force to be covered, the proximity of the enemy, the probability of attack, the time required by the troops protected to come into action in case of attack, the distance of the outposts from those troops, and the nature of the ground. It lies with the outpost commander to decide whether any of the troops allotted to him shall be used as a reserve.

150. *Duties of the commander of an outpost company.*

1. Outpost companies provide piquets, detached posts, and supports as required.

2. The commander of an outpost company, having received his orders, will move his command, taking precautions against surprise, to the ground allotted to it, where the men will be halted under cover.

3. He will then examine the ground, decide on the number and position of the piquets and, if necessary, of detached posts, required by day and by night, and on the position of the support. He will give instructions to the commanders of piquets and detached posts, and will arrange for a protracted resistance to be made on the line occupied by the piquets, which must correspond generally with the outpost line of resistance indicated by the outpost commander, and should support, and be supported by, the companies on either flank.

4. As soon as the piquets are in position and their groups and sentries posted, he will withdraw the covering troops. Such troops as are required for night dispositions only should not be posted till after dusk.

5. If it is necessary to send out patrols (*see* Sec. **156**) he will make the required arrangements, deciding whether they should be furnished by piquets or supports. When the troops who covered the company's advance to the outpost position are available it is sometimes convenient that they, who already know something of the country in front, should be detailed for this duty.

6. He will communicate with the companies on the flanks of his position, and will ascertain the dispositions of those companies, so as to ensure no ground being unprotected. He will also maintain communication with the outpost commander.

7. Piquets, detached posts, and supports will as far as possible be composed of complete units, the supports consisting of those platoons or sections not required for piquets and detached posts.

8. The distance of the support from the piquets will depend on the ground. The support should be able to reinforce the piquet line rapidly when required, yet should be far enough away to prevent the men's rest being unnecessarily disturbed.

9. When the company is watching a very extensive front it may be advisable to divide the support into two or more parts, or to detail a support to each piquet.

10. Communications between supports and piquets should be marked out in such a way that they can be followed easily at night without confusion. Every man of the support should be told exactly what he is to do in case of attack,

and should be required, while daylight lasts, to get a clear mental picture of his surroundings.

11. Supports will maintain communication with their piquets, and, if there is one, with the reserve.

151. *Duties of a piquet commander.*

1. As soon as a piquet commander has received his orders he will move his command, by a covered approach, if possible, to a spot in rear of the portion of the piquet line for which he is responsible. He will then examine the ground and decide on the number and position of sentry groups required, both by day and by night, remembering that no more should be used than are absolutely necessary. By day, in open country, one sentry over the piquet, and one sentry group in front of it may often be all that is required. He will then explain his orders to the piquet and will detail the various duties and their reliefs, including one or more single sentries over the piquet itself, for the purpose of communicating with the sentry groups and warning the piquet in case of attack. Sentry groups required only for night dispositions will not be posted till after dusk.

2. In order to prevent the men being unnecessarily disturbed at night, he will arrange that the non-commissioned officers and men of each relief of the various duties bivouac together, and apart from the other reliefs. All reliefs should know exactly where to find the men of the next relief.

3. He will satisfy himself that every man of his piquet knows the direction of the enemy, the position of the next piquets, and of the support, and what he is to do in case of attack by day or by night. He will then post his sentry groups, satisfying himself that no portion of the frontage

allotted to him is left unwatched, and will instruct sentries and commanders of sentry groups on the points enumerated in Sec. **152.**

4. He will strengthen the position to be defended, providing accommodation for the support as well as the piquet, and will improve communications where necessary, without waiting for orders on these points, and will make the necessary sanitary arrangements.

5. He will impress on his men the importance, where possible, of getting a clear mental picture of their surroundings while daylight lasts, so that they may the more easily find their way about by night.

6. He will maintain communication with the piquets on either flank, arranging with them for mutual support ; and while limiting as much as possible any movements in the line of sentries which might be visible to an enemy, he will satisfy himself that the sentries are alert and understand their duties.

7. Piquets will invariably be ready for action. By night the men must never lay aside their accoutrements.

8. Not more than a few men should be allowed to leave the piquet for any purpose at one time. They should never be allowed to move about in or in front of the sentry line when seeking water, fuel, forage, &c.

152. *Sentries and sentry groups.*

1. Sentries in the front line are posted in groups, which consist of from three to eight men under a non-commissioned officer or the oldest soldier. These groups remain on duty for eight or twelve hours, and thus require no reliefs when the force is only halting for the night. In open country one man is posted as sentry, while the remainder

lie down close at hand ; but if the country is close, or special precautions are necessary, the sentry post may be doubled. Sentries should always be posted double when men are very tired.

2. The distance of a sentry post from the piquet depends entirely upon the ground. Sentries should be placed so as to gain a clear view over the ground in their front, whilst concealed from the enemy's view. To avoid attracting attention, they should not be permitted to move about ; on the other hand permission to lie down, except to fire, should only be given for special reasons, since sentries permitted to lie down may not remain sufficiently alert. Sentries must be made to realise the importance of their work, and their eyes and ears must always be ready to catch any indication of the presence or the movement of the enemy.   Except at night, or in a fog, the bayonets of sentries should not be fixed.

3. On the approach of any person or party, a sentry will immediately warn his group.   When the nearest person is within speaking distance the sentry will call out *Halt*, take cover himself, and get ready to fire.   Any person not obeying the sentry, or attempting to make off after being challenged, will be fired upon without hesitation.   If the order to halt is obeyed, the group commander will order the person, or one of the party, to advance and give an account of himself.

4. Sentries must know, in addition to the points mentioned in Sec. **151** :—

    i. The direction of the enemy.

    ii. The position of the sentries on their right and left.

    iii. The position of the piquet, of neighbouring piquets, and of any detached post in the neighbourhood.

    iv. The ground they have to watch.

>   v. How they are to deal with persons approaching their posts.
>
>   vi. Whether any friendly patrols or scouts may be expected to return through their portion of the line, and the signal, if any, by which they may be recognised.

and, by day—

>   vii. The names of all villages, rivers, &c., in view, and the places to which roads and railways lead.

Commanders of sentry groups must in addition know what is to be done with persons found entering or leaving the outpost line (*see* Sec. **153**). They must also be given explicit orders what to do in case of an advance in force by the enemy : whether they are to remain at their posts, which in this case must be protected from fire from behind as well as from the front, or whether they are to retire on the piquet. In the latter case they must be warned of the danger of arriving headlong on the piquet only just ahead of the enemy. In consequence of this danger such retirements are rarely permissible at night.

153. *Traffic through the outposts.*

1. No one other than troops on duty, prisoners, deserters, and flags of truce will be allowed to pass through the outposts either from within or from without, except with the authority of the commander who details the outposts. Inhabitants with information will be blindfolded and detained at the nearest piquet pending instructions, and their information sent to the outpost commander.

2. No one is allowed to speak, otherwise than as directed in Sec. **152** (3), to persons presenting themselves at the outpost

line, except the commander of the nearest detached post,
piquet, or outpost company, who should confine his conversation to what is essential. Prisoners and deserters will
be sent at once, under escort, through the commander of the
outpost company, to the outpost commander.

154. *Flags of truce.*

1. On the approach of a flag of truce, one sentry, or more
if at hand, will advance and halt it at such distance as to
prevent any of the party who compose it overlooking the
posts; he will detain the flag of truce until instructions
are received from the commander of the outpost company.

2. If permission is given for it to pass the outposts, the
individuals bearing it must first be blindfolded, and then led
under escort to the outpost commander. No conversation
except by his permission is to be allowed on any subject,
under any pretence, with the persons bearing the flag of
truce.

3. If the flag of truce is merely the bearer of a letter or
parcel, the commander of the outpost company must receive
it, and instantly forward it to headquarters. The flag of truce,
having taken a receipt, will be required forthwith to depart,
and no one must be allowed to hold any conversation with
the party.

155. *Detached posts.*

1. Detached posts from an outpost company may occasionally be necessary in front of, or to the extreme flank of, the
line of resistance, to guard some spot where the enemy might
collect preparatory to an attack, or which he might occupy
for purposes of observation. They should only be employed

in exceptional circumstances, owing to the danger of their being cut off.

2. The strength of a detached post will depend on the duty required of it, and may vary from a section to a platoon.

3. Detached posts act in the manner laid down for piquets and sentry groups. When only required for night dispositions they should not be posted till after dusk.

156. *Outpost patrols.*

1. The duty of observation as defined in Sec. **147,** 3 will be carried out principally by means of patrols or standing patrols (*see* para. 7 below).

2. Movements of patrols through the outpost line should be as few as is consistent with the performance of this duty. By day movements through the outpost line may disclose the dispositions of the outposts, while by night there is great danger of returning patrols being shot by their own side.

3. Whether mounted troops from the outpost line are patrolling to the front or not, every commander of an outpost company is responsible for his own protection against surprise. He will be informed by the outpost commander as to what mounted patrols have been sent out, and must then decide what further patrols, if any, are necessary for his own security, having due regard to the principle enunciated in para. 2 above. When mounted troops are in front it should seldom be necessary to send out infantry patrols by day unless the country is very thick or the weather misty. By night the majority of mounted troops will be withdrawn, a few standing patrols only being left out to watch either the enemy or distant points by which he might approach,

and increased vigilance will then be necessary on the part of outpost companies.

In the absence of definite orders piquet commanders are responsible for taking such action as they deem necessary for the security of their piquets.

4. Outpost patrols, whether mounted or dismounted, may consist of from three to eight men under a non-commissioned officer. They should never be sent out in such regular sequence as will enable the enemy to foresee their movements. If a force halts more than one day in the same place the hours at which the patrols go out (except those before sunrise, *see* para. 6), and also their route, should be changed daily.

5. An outpost patrol, when going out, informs the nearest sentry of the direction it is taking and arranges some signal by which it may be recognised on its return. In the event of a patrol not returning when expected, another should be sent out. (*See also* Sec. **111.**)

6. When mounted troops are available they should move out before it begins to get light and patrol all approaches within distant field artillery range of the outposts. When mounted troops are not available infantry patrols should be sent out at this time, but it will seldom be advisable for them to reconnoitre so far from the outpost position. These patrols must remain out till after daybreak.

7. A standing patrol is a patrol sent out to remain at some definite spot to watch either the enemy, a road by which he might advance, or a locality where he could concentrate unseen. Standing patrols may be furnished by mounted troops or infantry. They are of the utmost value, especially at night, as they obviate constant movement. A standing patrol must be prepared to remain out for several hours. Its commander must arrange to send back an imme-

diate report of any hostile movement observed, and, if the enemy advances in strength, he must in default of other orders, retire on the piquet line before becoming seriously engaged.

157. *Battle outposts.*

1. If the enemy is close at hand, and battle imminent, or if the battle ceases only at nightfall to be renewed next day, the whole of the troops must be in complete readiness for action. There may not even be room for outposts, and the troops will have to bivouac in their battle positions, protected only by patrols and sentries. In such cases the firing line takes the place of the piquets. It will often occur in these circumstances that no orders can be issued as to measures of protection by superior authority, and in any case nothing can relieve the commanders of advanced battalions and companies of the responsibility of securing themselves from surprise, and, unless circumstances forbid, of keeping touch with the enemy.

CHAPTER XV.

MACHINE GUNS IN BATTLE.

158. *Characteristics of machine guns.*

1. A machine gun in action requires a frontage of about two yards. From this narrow front it can deliver a fire equal in volume to that of about 30 men firing rapidly, the frontage required for the latter being at least 15 times as great. It is therefore easier to find a concealed position for a machine gun than for the number of riflemen required to produce an equal volume of fire.

2. When well concealed the gun offers a difficult target, and, as only two men are required for its service, it is not put out of action should these become casualties, provided the remainder of the detachment are trained to take their places.

3. As regards fire effect :—

    i. The effective range of the machine gun may be taken as equal to that of the rifle.

    ii. It has been found by experiment that the fire of a machine gun is about twice as concentrated as that of riflemen firing an equal number of rounds at the same target.

4. In the important matter of control of fire the machine gun has several advantages. Once the gun is loaded and laid, fire can be turned on or off instantaneously ; it can be directed as readily as required and can be distributed laterally by traversing.

5. By mounting a few men on the limbered wagon, the guns can be moved rapidly from place to place, while a machine gun with tripod mounting can be taken wherever men on foot can go.

6. On the other hand the machine gun has certain disadvantages as compared with riflemen :—

    i. It is more defenceless when on the move, whether carried in the limbered wagon or on pack transport.

    ii. Owing to the concentrated nature of its fire as compared with a similar amount of rifle fire, the effect of small errors in aiming or elevation is greater. Thus, a comparatively small error at effective or long ranges will cause the fire of a machine gun to miss altogether a target which would probably be struck by several shots from riflemen making the same error in aim or elevation.

    iii. The mechanism of the gun is liable to temporary interruption.

    iv. The peculiar noise of the automatic firing attracts attention to the gun, and when steam is given off, owing to the water in the barrel casing boiling, the position of the gun can be readily located unless well concealed.

159. *General principles of the employment of infantry machine guns.*

1. The general principles governing the employment of machine guns are based upon the characteristics described in the previous section.

2. (i) The machine gun is a powerful auxiliary to, and well adapted for close co-operation with, infantry.

(ii) The concentrated and accurate nature of its fire, and
the speed with which it can be directed on the
objective, suits it for the development of surprise
effect and covering fire at effective and close infantry
ranges.

(iii) The small frontage which it occupies makes it valuable in cramped localities such as salients, villages,
roads, or defiles, where it is not possible to deploy a
number of rifles. It can also be usefully employed
to bring a concentrated enfilade fire to bear on a
definite line, such as a hedge, wall, or line of obstacles.

(iv) The power of opening fire at any time when the gun is
once laid is valuable on outpost or for night firing, for
the gun can command any required locality for any
length of time, and it is only necessary to press the
double button to produce and apply a large volume
of accurate fire at the moment it is required.

(v) The power of turning rapidly in any desired direction,
or of "all-round traverse," enables the gun to be
brought to bear upon a fresh target without moving
the tripod, and with the minimum of movement
and exposure. The machine gun can therefore
engage quickly an enemy advancing from an unexpected direction without increasing its vulnerability
to enfilade fire. This suits it for employment on a
flank, in a detached post, or to support infantry
in meeting an enveloping attack.

(vi) The power of accompanying infantry in any nature of
country is particularly useful in close country. The
mobility of the limbered wagons allows the guns to
be used to meet unexpected or critical situations so

that they may often be usefully employed as a mobile reserve of fire, when they can be moved unseen.

3. The usefulness of the machine gun is limited by its characteristics in the following way :—

    i. It is difficult to observe its fire accurately at long ranges, and as compared with field guns its ranging power is limited. It cannot therefore be considered as suitable, normally, for use in place of or as an addition to artillery.

    ii. Owing to the concentration of its fire, the expenditure of ammunition is likely to be out of proportion to the results obtained against small or scattered targets such as extended infantry. Unless the range can be ascertained accurately, or the target has considerable depth, effect can only be ensured at ranges of over 1,200 yards by the skilful fire direction of several guns and a heavy expenditure of ammunition.

    iii. Owing to the liability of the mechanism to interruption and the expenditure of ammunition involved, the gun is not suited for sustained fire action.

4. To sum up, machine guns are essentially weapons of opportunity. The power of the gun is best used to develop unexpected bursts of fire against favourable targets.

160. *The organization and tactical handling of infantry machine guns.*

1. Machine guns are organized in sections, which form an integral part of the battalions to which they belong. But as circumstances will often make it advisable to employ several sections together, a brigade commander may detach two or

more machine gun sections temporarily from their battalions and place them under the brigade machine gun officer (*see* Sec. 8), for employment as a unit of the brigade.

2. When employed by sections with their battalions machine guns are usually better able to take advantage of fleeting opportunities to support infantry closely, and are more easily concealed both on the move and in action, than when brigaded.

On the other hand a single section of these guns cannot be relied upon to obtain results proportionate to the expenditure of ammunition, when first opening fire, at distances beyond about 1,200 yards. Further, it is rarely possible to arrange that sections acting independently shall co-operate effectively with each other.

3. By employing several sections under the control of one commander a brigade commander is able to keep a powerful reserve of fire in hand to be used for any special purpose, the probability of obtaining good effect at ranges beyond 1,200 yards is increased, and it is easier to ensure that the fire is directed on the objective desired by the brigade commander.

4. The disadvantages of brigading machine guns are :—
    (i) That the difficulties of concealment are increased.
    (ii) That at shorter ranges than 1,000 yards the control of more than one section usually becomes difficult, more especially in attack.
    (iii) That the positions suitable for a number of sections in attack are often difficult to find at effective and close ranges, and that the combined movement of a number of sections is only possible under such conditions when the ground is very favourable.

5. It will, therefore, usually depend upon the general situation and upon the ground how many machine guns should be

placed under the control of the brigade machine gun officer, and how many left with the battalions to which they belong.

6. In attack, when the facilities for concealment and control at effective range are good, good results may be obtained by unity of command, and, by a timely concentration of fire, machine guns may be an important factor in the struggle for superiority of fire.

When control and concealment are difficult, or when the brigade is extended over a wide front, it will usually be better to leave guns with their units.

It will often be advisable to employ both methods and to leave their own machine guns with the battalions which are first extended, while those of battalions in reserve are placed under the command of the brigade machine gun officer.

7. Machine guns will usually find opportunities for employment in the attack, in assisting the advance of their infantry by means of covering fire, in protecting attacking infantry against counter-attack or against cavalry, in covering an exposed flank, in assisting the infantry in the fire fight, in preparing for the assault by sudden bursts of fire against the objective of the attack, and in assisting to secure localities seized during the advance. After a successful assault machine guns should reach the captured position as soon as possible in order to pursue the enemy with fire and cover the re-forming of their infantry. In the event of an assault being unsuccessful machine guns should cover the retirement of their own troops, if necessary sacrificing themselves in order to do so.

8. Once in action machine guns should change position as seldom as possible. The difficulties of ranging and of concealment on the move usually outweigh the advantages of decreasing the range.

9. In defence machine guns permanently allotted to the defensive line may lose their mobility, and can rarely be used as a reserve of fire for special purposes, since it is not possible to foresee the action of the enemy when allotting them to their positions. For these reasons it should be exceptional to employ more than a limited number of guns with the firing line in a defensive position. It is better to reconnoitre and prepare machine gun positions, and to keep the bulk of the guns out of action and in hand until an opportunity occurs for using them with a reasonable prospect of decisive effect. It is easy to detach guns where required if they are held in hand, but when distributed and in position it is less easy to collect and withdraw them.

When employed with the firing line in a defensive position, machine guns may be used either dispersed, or brigaded to command approaches, defiles, exits from woods, &c., and to bring fire to bear upon the ground in front of weak parts of the position.

10. When retained as part of a local reserve, machine guns retain their mobility and are therefore available to meet any unexpected situation, or to support local counter attacks closely.

In order to make full use of the guns alternative positions should be allotted to sections. These positions should be thoroughly reconnoitred and all necessary arrangements made for rapid occupation and quick opening of fire.

These arrangements should include :—Previous preparation of cover, information as to the shortest route to the various positions, preparation of range cards, selection of the most suitable position from which to control and observe fire, the most suitable position for the limbered wagons, and arrangements for the supply of ammunition and water.

11. Owing to the liability of the mechanism to interruption, the guns of a section should rarely be employed beyond supporting distance of one another ; when sections are acting independently and good cover is not available the guns should usually be not less than 25 yards apart, the average width of the area of ground struck by the bullets of an effective shrapnel.

12. As a general principle no more guns should fire than are necessary to meet the tactical requirements, the remainder being placed in concealed positions ready to open fire on a favourable opportunity or held in positions of readiness under cover according to circumstances. It is, however, of the first importance that sufficient fire effect to attain the object in view should be produced.

13. A machine gun commander should be given definite orders by the commander of the body of troops to which he belongs, as to what is required of him, but he should be allowed as much freedom of action as possible in carrying out these orders, and should be kept informed of all changes and developments of the situation which may affect his action. Initiative and enterprise are essential to the effective handling of machine guns.

14. Machine guns will usually be sufficiently protected by the dispositions of the troops with whom they are acting. Should a machine gun commander find himself in an exposed position, he should apply to the nearest infantry commander for a suitable escort if necessary.

15. When a machine gun is in action only those numbers required to work the gun should be with it. Spare numbers, when not employed as range takers, ground scouts, ammunition carriers, or on similar duties, should be under cover in the vicinity. Groups of men close to machine guns hinder the

working of the gun, are apt to disclose its position, and make a vulnerable target.

The limbered wagons will be unpacked in positions where they are screened from the enemy's fire and observation.

The commander of the machine gun section will arrange for the selection of a covered position for his small arm ammunition cart, as close to his guns as possible.

161. *Choice of fire positions.*

1. *Reconnaissance.* — Surprise and concealment being important factors in the employment of machine guns, their effective use depends largely upon the skill with which they have been brought into action.

Reconnaissance is therefore of special importance. The brigade machine gun officer if the guns are brigaded, the section officer if they are not, accompanied by range takers and orderlies, should usually be well in advance of his guns, where he can observe the action of the body of infantry with which he is co-operating. He should carefully reconnoitre suitable fire positions and make all preparations for bringing his guns rapidly into action. Alternative positions to which the guns may be moved to meet changes in the situation or to avoid artillery fire should always be selected.

Similar reconnaissances should be carried out, whenever possible, before changing position.

2. The choice of a fire position must depend upon the tactical requirements of the situation, and upon the object in view ; for example, it must depend upon whether it is desired to use covering, enfilade, or flanking fire, or to act by surprise.

In undulating or mountainous country it may be possible to provide covering fire from positions in rear, but in flat country it will rarely be possible to fire over the heads of men in front, and fire positions for machine guns must be sought on the flanks.

Except when affording covering fire from the rear, the gun should be sited as low as is compatible with obtaining the necessary field of fire.

3. A clear field of fire, facilities for observation, a covered approach, concealment and cover for the guns and their detachments, and facilities for ammunition supply, are advantages to be looked for in a good fire position, but one position will rarely unite them all.   As a general principle, when the situation calls for effective fire, fire effect must not be sacrificed to obtain concealment.

In arranging for the concealment of the guns it is important to consider the background.   The neighbourhood of landmarks and the tops of prominent features should be avoided.

162. *General principles of fire control.*

1. The general considerations which govern the selection of a target for machine guns are, its tactical importance, its range, and its vulnerability.

2. Machine guns should rarely open fire except :—

  i. To facilitate movement of their own infantry.
  ii. To prevent or delay movement of the enemy.
  iii. Against a favourable target.

As soon as a machine gun opens fire its presence may be disclosed ; its subsequent appearance will then be watched for, and it loses to a great extent the advantage of surprise. Fire should, therefore, not be opened without good reason.

Again, fire should not be opened at ranges beyond 1,200 yards unless a particularly favourable target offers, or a number of guns can be employed (*see* Sec. **160**, 3). Between 1,200 and 800 yards good effect may be anticipated from machine gun fire, and within 800 yards the greatest possible effect should be developed. If the firer can himself obtain observation, the effect of machine gun fire is appreciably increased.

3. Except under special circumstances, as for example when the tactical situation demands the opening of fire irrespective of the probability of obtaining material results in hits, machine guns should open fire only upon targets which are sufficiently large and dense to promise an adequate return for the ammunition expended. Thin lines of infantry in extended order are not a suitable target.

If there is no satisfactory indication of effect, and no special justification for firing at long range exists, it will usually be better to withdraw from action and to seek other opportunities for effective intervention.

4. Machine guns should seldom engage artillery with direct fire beyond close rifle range, for in such circumstances superiority of fire will always rest with the artillery if the machine guns are located. Within close rifle range machine guns, if concealed, should inflict considerable loss on artillery.

5. To sum up, fire should only be opened when probable results will justify it, and the tactical situation demands it. When opened, fire should be maintained so long as there is a reasonable chance of attaining the object for which it was opened. The method and volume of fire must be determined by the tactical situation, the object in view, the nature of the target, the nature of the ground, and the characteristics of the gun.

If these results are to be attained fire must be skilfully controlled and directed by machine gun commanders.

6. When two or more sections are brigaded they will act as a unit under the command of the brigade machine gun officer, who, if the conditions are favourable, *i.e.*, if the sections can be brought into action in such a way that his orders can be heard clearly by all concerned, will direct the fire as regards range, point of aim, method of fire, and the opening and cessation of fire.

It will, however, seldom be possible for a brigade machine gun officer to make his voice heard by more than one section of guns, and the orders for fire direction will usually be limited to indicating the objective by signal or message, and to ordering the opening and cessation of fire, all other details being left to the section officers.   High training in semaphore and in the correct passing of orders is essential.

163. *Methods of fire.*

1. The principal methods of fire are :—
   i. Ranging fire.
   ii. Rapid fire.
   iii. Traversing fire.

i. In *Ranging fire* groups of from 10 to 20 rounds are used to obtain observation.   When the conditions for observation are favourable a group of 10 rounds should be sufficient.   Under less favourable conditions, groups of as many as 20 rounds may be necessary, but if observation is not then obtained it is unlikely to be obtained with larger groups.   Single deliberate shots are of no value for ranging. Ranging fire should never be used when surprise is of importance.

ii. *Rapid fire* is used when the greatest volume of fire is required. It is produced and applied by means of a series of long groups of from 30 to 50 rounds. The firer pauses momentarily between each group to ensure that the sights are correctly aligned, and continues until ordered to cease fire or until he considers it necessary to do so. Rapid fire will be used (1) when the sighting elevation has been successfully obtained by ranging fire ; (2) when surprise effect is required ; (3) with combined sights.

iii. *Traversing fire.*—This method is employed against a linear target, and is applied by means of a series of small groups with the object of covering as wide a front as possible with only sufficient volume to ensure effect. In this case a group should consist of from 5 to 10 rounds only, because against a linear target greater volume will not produce greater effect. (*See also* Sec. **103**, 10.) Traversing may be either horizontal or diagonal.

2. *Combined sights.*—When two or more guns are working together, the depth of the effective zone can be increased by ordering different elevations to be used by each gun, while each uses the same aiming mark. By this means, while the effective zone is increased, the density of fire is considerably reduced. The difference of elevation used depends chiefly on the number of guns available. For general guidance, when one section only is available, combined sights differing by 100 yards should be used at and beyond 800 yards and up to 1,200 yards inclusive ; beyond 1,200 yards the difference in sighting should not exceed 50 yards between guns. With two or more sections the difference of sighting between guns should not exceed 50 yards. When both guns of a section are sighted to the same elevation, " combined sights by sections," differing by 100 yards may be used.

Combined sights should at once be discontinued if accurate observation of the strike of bullets can be obtained.

Machine gun commanders when ordering combined sights will give out the lowest range and the difference in sighting to be used. The lowest range will always be taken by the left hand gun of the section or sections as the case may be. The No. 1 of that gun will pass to the No. 1 of the gun on his right the range he himself is using and the difference ordered, and so on down the line.

When the target to be engaged is a narrow one, and all guns are using the same aiming mark, it will generally be impossible for the firers to observe their own particular cone of fire. In these circumstances no alteration in sighting is permissible except under the orders of the machine gun commander. In other circumstances, *i.e.*, when the guns are laid on different points of aim, each firer should endeavour to correct his elevation from observation of the bullet strike. In such cases the effect may be increased by traversing from the flanks inwards, or from the centre outwards. If, as a result of his observations or for other reasons, the machine gun commander wishes to alter the sighting, the quickest method is to bring the elevation of the left hand gun above that of the right hand gun or to lower the elevation of the right hand gun below that of the left hand gun according as to whether he wishes to increase or decrease the elevation. If the machine gun commander is directing the fire from the opposite flank to that of the gun or guns whose elevation he wishes to alter, it will be necessary to cease firing momentarily for his order to be received, after which he will immediately give the signal to continue. This will often not be necessary when he is on the same flank.

164. *Signals.*

1. In many cases observation will be impossible from the gun position, and it will be necessary for observers to signal results from a flank.

The following semaphore code is used in signalling the results of observation of fire :—

P = Plus : meaning fire observed at least 50 yards beyond target.

M = Minus : meaning fire observed at least 50 yards short of target.

T = Right : meaning fire observed to right of target.

L = Left :   ,,   ,,   ,,   to left of target.

C = Centre :   ,,   direction of fire correct.

U = Unobserved : meaning no observation obtained.

Q = Query : meaning fire observed but its position uncertain.

R = Range : meaning range correct.

2. The signaller at the observation post should give the " call up " to show that the observers are ready. " P " ; and " M " may be repeated for multiples of 50 yards, thus " P P " would mean, " fire observed at least 100 yards beyond target." Signals should be repeated from the gun position if this can be done without disclosing the position to the enemy.

3. On all occasions when guns are firing, the following signals should be used in controlling fire :—

Signal for " action."—Both arms, fully extended, raised from the sides to a position in line with the shoulders and lowered again. This motion to be repeated until it is seen that the signal is being complied with.

Signal for " out of action."—Arms swung in a circular
    motion in front of the body.
By No. 2.   Hand up = Gun ready to open fire.
By Controlling Officer.   Hand up = Preparatory to
                      opening fire.
                      Hand dropped = Open fire.
                      Elbow close to the side,
                      forearm waved horizontally
                      = Cease fire.
Other signals as in Sec. **94.**

CHAPTER XVI.

AMMUNITION SUPPLY. ENTRENCHING TOOLS.

165. *Method of conveying ammunition from the base to the battlefield.*

1. The administrative services deliver ammunition at the "Refilling Points," which are situated within reach of the fighting troops, usually within one day's march of them (Field Service Regulations, Part I, and Part II, Sec. 49).

2. The reserves* of ammunition held by fighting troops are divided into three lines :—

    (i) Divisional ammunition column reserve.

    (ii) Artillery brigade ammunition column reserve.

    (iii) Regimental reserve.

The amount of ammunition carried in each line is published in War Establishments.

3. The divisional ammunition columns, which connect the artillery brigade ammunition columns with the administrative services at the refilling points, usually march in accordance with orders received from divisional headquarters, and when an action is imminent push sections forward to connect with their artillery brigade ammunition columns. (Field Service Regulations, Part I, and Field Artillery Training.)

---

* In India the reserves of ammunition held by fighting troops are divided into three lines—(i) Divisional ammunition column reserve, (ii) Regimental reserve, (iii) Section reserve. The principles of ammunition supply are the same as those given in this chapter.

4. The artillery brigade ammunition columns, in each of which a section is allotted to carry ammunition for one infantry brigade, furnish the second reserve of small arm ammunition.

In an emergency in action ammunition from these columns must be supplied to any troops on demand, but normally the infantry brigade which each is to supply is detailed so that the column commanders may know whom they have to supply and each infantry brigade know whence to expect replenishment.

These artillery brigade ammunition columns usually march immediately in rear of the fighting troops of their respective divisions, unless circumstances render this undesirable. During an action they are established by artillery brigade commanders in positions favourable for communication and movement, about one mile from the position of the line of guns, the columns being split up into sections should the wide extension of the troops to be supplied render such a course necessary.

5. The artillery brigade ammunition column commanders on approaching the battlefield will :—

> (i) Send forward an officer or non-commissioned officer to ascertain the position of the troops which he has to supply.
>
> (ii) Detach an orderly to remain with the commander of the infantry brigade ammunition reserve (*see* Sec. **166**) until there is no longer any probability of ammunition being required.
>
> (iii) During the action send forward ammunition as demanded by the commander of the infantry brigade ammunition reserve. The transport conveying this ammunition will normally be unloaded

and returned to the brigade ammunition column as soon as possible. When the ammunition is carried in S.A.A. carts it is transferred as a rule to the empty darts, which are withdrawn if necessary to a covered position for the purpose. Should this not be feasible the artillery teams may be transferred to, and return with, the empty carts.

166. *The direct issue from and replenishment of the battalion S.A.A. carts and pack animals.*

1. The small arm ammunition available in an infantry battalion consists of :—

120 rounds carried by the soldier.

100 rounds, regimental reserve, carried for each rifle partly on eight pack animals (two per company) and the remainder either in S.A.A. carts or on pack animals*.

3,500 rounds are carried in the limbered wagons of the machine gun section. 8,000 rounds reserve ammunition are carried in the S.A.A. cart of the section.

2. A brigade reserve, under a selected officer, will normally be formed by detaching from each battalion as much of its

---

* In Expeditionary Force and Territorial Force War Establishments each battalion has five S.A.A. carts in addition to the company pack animals and the ammunition cart of the machine gun section.

The whole of the ammunition allotted to infantry battalions in "War Establishments," India, is carried on pack transport.

In India the number of rounds differ, chiefly owing to the requirements of pack transport, but the principles are the same, the brigade reserve being formed by detaching a portion of the regimental reserve The section reserve always remains with companies.

regimental reserve ammunition as the brigade commander may think fit. The brigade reserve forms a link between the regimental reserve and the artillery brigade ammunition column. It should be regarded as available for the brigade generally, but in the case of necessity it will supply ammunition to any troops engaged. This reserve marches in rear of the brigade and during an action moves as the brigade commander may direct. It should be accompanied by orderlies to maintain communication with the various regimental reserves.

If battalions are detached to any distance, they will usually take the whole of their regimental reserves with them, the brigade reserve being re-formed on their return.

3. The commander of the brigade ammunition reserve will :—

    i. Open up communication with the artillery brigade ammunition column and also with the various regimental reserves.

    ii. Take the earliest opportunity to fill up empty transport from the artillery brigade ammunition column. The request for the amount of ammunition required will be sent, in writing, to the officer in charge of the small arm ammunition section of the artillery brigade ammunition column by the artillery orderly furnished for that purpose, who will also act as guide to the officer bringing the ammunition forward. This orderly will be used for no other purpose. When the ammunition is carried in S.A.A. carts, the number of full carts required will be demanded, in other cases the required number of boxes.

   iii. Not send men and transport animals belonging to the brigade reserve to the artillery brigade ammunition column, nor men and transport animals belonging to the latter further to the front than the brigade reserve, except in case of emergency.

   iv. Retain empty transport in the brigade reserve until reloaded or replaced.

   v. Sign receipts prepared by the officer in charge of the artillery brigade ammunition column for the number of full carts received, if the ammunition is forwarded in S.A.A. carts, or for the number of full ammunition boxes if the ammunition is forwarded by other transport.

   vi. After an action or during a pause in the engagement make good from the artillery brigade ammunition column all deficiences of ammunition.

4. The ammunition transport remaining with each battalion after the brigade reserve has been formed marches in rear of the battalion, or as the brigade commander may direct.

5. Whenever a collision with the enemy is probable battalion commanders will, on their own initiative, increase the number of rounds carried by each man to 200 from their regimental reserves, taking the necessary steps to replenish their reserves as soon as possible from the brigade reserve. It will usually be advisable to issue these extra rounds from the portion of the regimental reserve not allotted to companies.

6. On deployment the transport carrying the machine gun ammunition moves as directed by the commander of the machine gun section. The portion of the regimental reserve not allotted to companies will be under the serjeant-major ; it will, at the outset, be retained in the hands of the battalion commander, and will move as directed by him. The exact

distribution in action of the regimental reserve must principally depend on the nature of the ground. The object is to
maintain the power of replenishing the supply from the brigade
reserve, whilst getting the regimental reserve as far forward
as possible so as to facilitate the supply of ammunition to
the firing line. The serjeant-major should be provided with
signallers and orderlies when necessary, for the purpose of
maintaining communication with the company pack animals
and with the brigade reserve. As the regimental reserve
becomes empty it will be refilled or exchanged, under the
direction of the serjeant-major, from the brigade reserve.
During the final stages of the attack every opportunity of
gaining ground must be seized, so that the regimental reserve
may be at hand as soon as the position is carried.

7. The ammunition pack animals allotted to companies join
their respective companies on the deployment of the battalion,
or when the companies are detached, and are then placed under
the charge of company quartermaster-serjeants. During an
action the company quartermaster-serjeant will direct the
movements of the pack animals in accordance with the orders
of the company commander and will keep as close to the company as possible. When men have once joined the firing line
they cannot be withdrawn to replenish ammunition except
under very favourable conditions of ground, and the ammunition of the firing line must therefore be replenished by reinforcing lines. Commanders of reinforcing troops will therefore
carefully watch the progress of the pack animals, and previous
to losing touch with these reserves will draw extra bandoliers
of ammunition for their own unit and for the firing line in
front. It will be the duty of the company quartermaster-
serjeants concerned to superintend the issue of this ammunition, and, as soon as the supply is exhausted, to return to

the regimental reserves for a further supply. When their own companies are absorbed in the firing line they will place their pack animals in the most favourable position for the issue of ammunition to the successive reinforcing troops. If more convenient, commanders of reinforcing troops may draw extra ammunition direct from the regimental reserves instead of from the company pack animals.

8. The amount of extra ammunition so issued to reinforcing troops must be dependent on :—

    i. The expenditure at the front.

    ii. The cover afforded by the ground to these reinforcements in their advance to the firing line.

    iii. The amount of ammunition which a man can carry without impairing his efficiency.

Open ground, in the face of a heavy fire, must be crossed by short rushes at top speed. For such an advance activity is the first consideration, and men should not be called upon to carry more than 300 rounds, except when the ground can be crossed in a single rush.

167.—*Entrenching implements and tools.**

1. An entrenching implement is carried by each private and N.C.O. up to the rank of serjeant inclusive.

The entrenching tools of a battalion are carried on two limbered G.S. wagons, each of which carries 8 felling axes, 4 hand axes, 38 picks, 4 crowbars, 20 bill hooks, 10 reaping hooks, and 5½ shovels. The second wagon carries 1 hand saw in addition.

---

*For a description of the entrenching implement and of entrenching tools *see* the " Manual of Field Engineering."

2 picks, 2 bill hooks, and 2 shovels are carried on the limbered wagon of the machine gun section.

A brigade reserve of entrenching tools is carried on two G.S. wagons, and consists of 1 hand axe, 368 picks, 9 crowbars, 3 reaping hooks, and 568 shovels.†

2. On the march the battalion tool wagons will march in rear of the battalion, or as the brigade commander may direct.

The brigade reserve of tools will remain with the brigade ammunition reserve and will be under the officer in charge of the latter.

---

† In India the entrenching tools of a battalion are carried on 8 pack animals. A brigade reserve of entrenching tools is not formed in normal conditions.

APPENDIX I.

Instruction in Bayonet Fighting.

1. *General instructions for bayonet fighting.*

1. The following instructions in bayonet fighting have been drawn up with the object of teaching men to use their bayonets with good effect in action.

2. A bayonet charge will normally be delivered in lines, possibly many deep, against a defending force also in lines, over rough ground, which may be covered with obstacles. Single combat will therefore be the exception, while fighting in mass will be the rule. This will make manœuvring for an opening impossible.

" In a bayonet fight the impetus of a charging line gives it moral and physical advantages over a stationary line. Infantry on the defensive should, therefore, always be ready to meet a bayonet charge by a counter-charge, if their fire fails to stop the assailant. This counter-charge, however, should not be made prematurely. The enemy cannot fire effectively and can rarely be well supported by covering fire while charging. He thus offers at such a time a very vulnerable target, of which advantage should be taken so long as a steady and well directed fire can be brought to bear on him. Should, however, the volume of fire be insufficient to check the assailant, a counter-charge must be made before he has actually reached the position. When it is made success will fall to the line which is best in hand and charges with most spirit and determination." (*See* Sec. **131, 4.**)

In teaching bayonet fighting individual instruction is essential ; some of the preliminary lessons, however, can be given in small squads. The best way to give the required individual instruction is by the method of " *Instructor and Pupil*," followed by two pupils opposing one another under the instructor's supervision, as is explained in the " Assaulting lessons."

To ensure individual instruction, it is desirable that not more than four pupils should be given to each instructor, and that the same instructor should take the same pupils throughout their course.

Every encouragement should be given to the men to practise bayonet fighting.*

3. The following lessons are arranged in progressive order and, in the first instance, should be taught in the order in which they are laid down.

Great importance should be attached to the Assaulting Lesson, as it is by means of it that the men are given a combative spirit and are enabled to see the fighting application of each detail which they are taught. The Assaulting Lesson should therefore be frequently practised by all, including skilled fighters, and, when once it has been learned, should always form part of a day's lesson.

Pupils should not be allowed to practise the actual " Assault " until they have had plenty of practice in the " Assaulting Lesson."

4. Suppleness, lightness, ease, and freedom of movement should be aimed at throughout the instruction, and all stiffness must be carefully avoided.

* Instruction in competition fighting is contained in " Instruction in Bayonet Fighting for Competitions."

It should be distinctly understood that the grasp of the rifle by either hand should never be released.

5. Great attention should be devoted to developing quickness, energy, and rapidity of movement. It is especially important to insist on a good and very rapid attack pushed well home. A resolute attack of this nature has far more chance of success than one that is not pushed with the same determination, and, even if it be parried, the very determination and energy with which it was delivered frequently so upsets the adversary that he is unable to "Return." A half-hearted attack is dangerous only to the attacker.

The training must also aim at developing the power of making a quick recovery after an attack has failed, and a good parry and return when attacked.

If the instruction be made progressive and lessons taught in the order here given, with repetition whenever necessary, the men should become efficient in the use of the bayonet and acquire a practical knowledge of its use in the combat.

6. Bayonet fighting should never be taught as a parade exercise.

When men are inspected in bayonet fighting, they should be seen at the Assault.

2. *Lesson* i.

Pupil with his own or D.P. rifle with bayonet fixed and enclosed in scabbard.

On Guard. Pl. XIX.	From the position of " Order Arms " cant the rifle forward, bayonet to the front, about as high as the breast, barrel inclining to the left and seize it with the left hand at the most convenient place below the lower band, but not below the back sight,

PLATE XVIII.   *To face p.* **224.**

THE POSITION "ON GUARD."

right hand grasping the ".small" and just
in advance of the hip.   Legs. in .a .natural·
position such ·as a man walking might
adopt on coming into collision with an
advancing enemy.

Great importance should be taken in training .men to. be
free from all stiffness and constraint so as to be ready for
instant movement of the rifle and body.   Allowance must .be
made for the difference in build of individual men, and
exact adherence to the typical position should not be required
so long as the principles indicated above are .adhered to,
i.e., easy balance of the body, forward threatening position
of the rifle covering the left side, and full control of the
weapon.

A spirit of aggression and alertness should show itself in
the position of On Guard.

The foregoing remarks apply to all the positions and
movements in Bayonet Fighting.

REST.
Without making a drill movement of it,
the pupil should assume a position of rest
from this or any other position in the
easiest way.

THE POINT.
Deliver the point as rapidly as possible
anywhere on the trunk to the full extent of
both arms, and withdraw the point at once..

N.B.—This should not be unduly hurried.   The instructor
must ensure speed both in delivering the point and its withdrawal, but great care must be taken to ensure a good " point "
before a quick withdrawal is made.   The body should .be
inclined forward so as to ensure its weight being behind the

point.   The left knee should be slightly bent rather than that the hips should be drawn back when delivering the point.

The pupil should now use the spring bayonet or, if this is unobtainable, a dummy rifle, and a left hand glove.

RIGHT
PARRY.
(HIGH OR
LOW.)

From the " On Guard " position, carry the rifle sufficiently to the right front straightening the left arm in doing so, so as to beat off the adversary's rifle to the right front.   In forming the parry the wrist should not be bent nor the rifle twisted in the hand.

LEFT
PARRY.
(HIGH OR
LOW.)

From the position of " On Guard " carry the rifle sufficiently to the left front, straightening the left arm in doing so, so as to beat off the adversary's rifle towards the left front ; and in the case of the low parry to the left front and downwards.

The left parry should be made with the barrel of the rifle to the left without bending the wrist or twisting the rifle round in the hand.   In forming the low parry, care should be taken not to raise the right hand.

The men should be taught to form the parries from any position.

The height from which the parries are made should, of course, vary according to the height of the adversary's attack.   In teaching the parries the instructor should at first illustrate them with the aid of an assistant who knows them.   He should then take each pupil separately, and by holding his weapon in the required position show him a threatening attack and make him parry it, indicating the part to be defended rather than the name of the parry.

By this means the pupil is made to realise from the beginning exactly what he has to parry, and the necessity for it.

Great care should be taken that the rifle is moved by the arms alone working free of the body, in other words, the body should not be thrown out of its normal position facing the adversary by following the movement of the rifle.

3. *Lesson* ii.

With Spring Bayonet practice " pointing " at " wall pad," " bag," or " dummy " under the following conditions :—

(*a*) From a stationary position.
(*b*) Taking a step forward.
(*c*) Walking up to it.

This is a very useful and important lesson in order to teach men to aim at and hit something with the point of the bayonet before being opposed to a living target. It also teaches them to judge their distance properly, and increases their speed and energy.

A " wall pad " can be made by hanging a padded jacket on the wall about the height of the breast of a man when " on guard " or by suspending a bag filled with paper, shavings, &c., having a rope fastened horizontally behind it to prevent it swinging away when hit.

N.B.—A pad fastened to a wall is not a good object at which to practice (*b*) and (*c*), there is too much shock from the resistance of the wall which causes the pupil to check as (or before) he delivers his point.

For a similar reason this lesson cannot be performed with a dummy rifle.

SHORTEN ARM.   { Draw the rifle sharply back horizontally to the full extent of the right arm, butt of the rifle either above or below the elbow.

From this position deliver the point as before, then return " on guard." This " point " is useful when the opponent is so close that it is not possible to use the bayonet in the ordinary way.

The pupil must be made to realise that whenever he fixes his " point " he will probably have to use considerable force to withdraw it, which will practically bring him into the " shorten arms " position. When withdrawing the point from, or threatening, an adversary close to him and below him, it will be noticed that the butt is brought backward below the elbow.

The " bag " used in Lesson ii may be suspended as already described or be made to stand on end on a bench (length-ways) in order to make it sufficiently high. The bag when filled should not be too light.

It is also a useful lesson to " point " at the bag on the ground (bag may be on end or lying down), the " shorten arms " being practised frequently when withdrawing the point.

4. *Lesson* iii.

Pupil with spring bayonet and left hand glove, instructor fully dressed.

PARRY AND RETURN.   { Instructor throws out his rifle as if he were going to make a point. Pupil parries sharply, and immediately returns, hitting the instructor.

Repeat in each line of attack, *i.e.*, the line in which the attack is made with reference to the opponent's weapon, taking care that the pupil shows sufficient opening (in whatever line it may be) for the instructor's attack.

In the above Lesson iii, both instructor and pupil are stationary.

N.B.—For the purposes of this lesson only, the instructor should have his rifle slightly drawn back in order that he may not be inside his pupil's guard, and the instructor must allow his body to move forward with his point when he " throws out his rifle."

5. *Lesson* iv.

Instructor and pupil fully dressed. A repetition of (c) in Lesson ii is advisable as a prelude to this Lesson iv.

DIRECT
ATTACK.

Instructor stands on guard facing pupil a few paces off. Instructor shows an opening. Pupil walks towards him and when within reach delivers a point on him wherever indicated ; he should be made to recover quickly ready to make another attack.

In order to avoid being injured by a point delivered at too close a range the instructor should ensure that the pupil does not deliver his point too late. If pupil delays his attack bayonets will be crossed before he begins to make his point, in which case the instructor should knock aside his bayonet, care being taken to inform him of the reason for so doing.

Each time the pupil fixes his point he must be made to realise that he would have to stop to withdraw it, by "shortening arms " if necessary. In order to make the pupil realise how necessary it is to do this with energy, the instructor should direct him to point under his right arm and should then grip the rifle, making him withdraw the point and shorten arms. He should also occasionally sink quickly to the ground and make the pupil withdraw the point from this position.

It should be impressed on the pupil that though his point has missed or has been parried, he can, as attacker, still maintain his advantage. Unless his adversary was at his mercy it would be impossible to shorten arms, but under real conditions he would employ any method of injuring his opponent, such as tripping, bringing up his knee quickly, &c., or making use of the :—

BUTT. { by bringing it up with a sharp jabbing motion done by raising it forward and upward with the right hand (right arm well bent, and right upper arm fairly close to the body, this ensures pupil closing up to adversary), at the same time assisting this movement by drawing the barrel of the rifle backwards over the left shoulder with the left hand.

The butt should only be used when the attack with the bayonet has failed, and it is impossible to use the point. It may be found more convenient, according to the direction in which the point has been parried, to use the butt horizontally on the adversary's left side, but it should be remembered that this may, in a charge, become a source of danger to comrades on the left.

TRIPPING.
{ Any form of tripping may be taught on mats. The use of the butt and tripping when known cannot be actually used in practising bayonet fighting.

Pupil should then be made to attack the instructor without knowing whether he will try to parry him or not ; utilising anything he may have been taught, according to circumstances.

It is not practical to show too large an opening in the " direct attack."

The " direct attack " can only be used on a living target in one line, i.e., where the instructor shows a " right opening."

If the instructor were to make a " left opening " which was in any way practical his point would during the whole time be on the pupil, who would be unable to take advantage of the opening without first knocking aside instructor's " point."

In the case of an attack at an " opening low " either the instructor has to show an unpractical and unnatural " opening " or else the pupil's attack is liable to injure the instructor, no matter whether he tries to parry it or not.

6. *Lesson* v.

Instructor and pupil fully dressed.

PARRY AND
RETURN,
as in
Lesson iv.
{ Pupil shows an opening on his right side and advances on instructor.

Instructor threatens an attack on pupil who parries and returns.

As already explained, this is done in one line only, as it is obvious that the pupil's point will so threaten the instructor in showing his " left opening " that the latter would not attempt to attack the pupil without first knocking aside his bayonet.

Pupil must be made to realise that the method of executing his return will depend on when the threatening attack is made by the instructor. If it is made soon (or too soon) the pupil will find that although he is advancing he has ample time for a " parry and return " ; but the longer the instructor delays his threatening attack the closer the pupil will be when he has to make his " return." Thus the lesson really devolves itself into the pupil parrying and then getting his " point on " as soon as possible, even " shortening arms " if necessary.

If the instructor delays his attack too long the pupil will be able to knock his rifle aside and make a " point " before the instructor can move.

7. *Lesson* vi.

Instructor and pupil fully dressed.

Lessons iv and v are repeated separately, but the instructor and pupil must advance towards each other.

In practising Lesson iv under these conditions, it will be found that it is not possible to perform the direct attack on the instructor without injuring him. As a substitute a sack suspended as in Lesson ii may be swung towards the pupil as he advances, thus teaching him to hit an object moving towards him. When he is sufficiently practised in this, the instructor may then take up his position and advance as indicated above, at the same time making pupil point at him so that he may catch the bayonet under his arm, making the pupil withdraw by " shortening arms," or he may also occasionally parry the pupil's attack, pupil being instructed to close on him as he did in Lesson iv when instructor was stationary.

If Lesson v is here done correctly it will be found that the only way the pupil can get his point on is by " shortening arms " and that the impetus of both advancing will carry his point through his adversary. A good parry and return might injure the instructor, but this should not occur so long as he does not threaten his attack too soon.

N.B.—It should be noted in all the foregoing lessons in which either the instructor or pupil or both advance, it must be carried out until both are in close contact.

8. *Lesson* vii.

Two pupils, both fully dressed, face each other about ten yards apart. On the word " Play " from the instructor both advance at the " walk."

ASSAULTING
LESSON.
" One " attacks direct, when within reach doing his best to hit his opponent.
" Other " endeavours to parry the attack. and, if he succeeds, to return at once. (This is then reversed, " one " becoming " other.")

It is difficult for " one " to hit " other " provided the latter shows only an ordinary, practical and natural " opening." If " one " finds he can get his point home on " other " it means (in all probability) that " other " is not trying to ward off " one's " bayonet as soon as it is within reach even if the latter has not begun to make his " point."

In this lesson each man knows what his opponent is trying to do, and there must be no attempt to deceive each other.

An attack must be made with speed and determination, and both pupils must do their best to hit.

If unsuccessful in his attack " one " should always endeavour to close on his opponent as in Lesson iv. If " other " is successful in his parry, he should at once try to return on his opponent, or threaten with the butt, &c. The fact that he knows that " one " will try and close on him emphasises the probability of his having to "shorten arms " to make his " return."

9. *Lesson* viii.

Two pupils dressed as in Lesson vii.

THE ASSAULT.
When the pupils have been sufficiently practised in the Assaulting Lesson, they should then place themselves about 30 yards apart, and on the word " charge," or on a whistle sounding, should double steadily forward at the " trail " : on nearing each other they should vigorously assault one another, utilising anything they may have been taught.

It should be impressed on the pupils that they must not stop in order to manœuvre for an " opening." Also that each must keep his point on the other and not show too big an opening.

The instructor who superintends this lesson must award the assault in favour of the pupil who gets in the first hit or whom the instructor thinks would have gained the advantage over the other.

The butt can only be used to threaten with here.   Pupils will soon learn to demonstrate the fact that they could have used the butt, &c., and instructor must watch carefully to see that the assault is not prolonged under impracticable conditions.

As there is danger to the pupils, great discretion must be used in practising the assault ; it should not be carried out more than once, and then only to illustrate the object of the previous lessons.

10. *Organization of the instruction in bayonet fighting.*

1. Company Officers.

Company officers are responsible for the training of their men in bayonet fighting.   They must therefore be efficient instructors.

2. N.C.Os. in Possession of Gymnastic Certificates.

Certificated gymnastic instructors (not Army Gymnastic Staff) will be made use of to assist in instructing young officers and other N.C.Os.

3. Non-Commissioned Officers.
(Other than certificated gymnastic instructors.)

All N.C.Os. will be instructed in the methods of giving the bayonet fighting lessons.

The best of these N.C.Os. will be selected to assist in the training of recruits.

4. Trained Soldiers.

The trained soldier will go through a short annual " refresher " course of bayonet fighting on the same lines as the recruit, under the direction of his company officers.   The duration of the course and the lessons given will be regulated according to the degree of proficiency of the individual.

APPENDIX II.

Syllabus for a Six Months' Course of Recruit Training.

1. The following syllabus of recruit training is given as a guide to officers charged with the training of recruits.   It is not intended that it should be followed rigidly.

2. Special Reserve recruits perform the first four months of the course.

1. Syllabus of training.

Employment.	Hours.	Remarks.
First Fortnight.		
Physical training ...	10	Physical training under qualified Instructors. (*See* " Manual of Physical Training.")
Squad drill without arms	17	For the first week it is recommended that all squad drill should be with intervals and in slow time only.
Musketry	10	
Lectures...	5	
Total	42	
Second Fortnight.		
Physical training ...	10	Physical training under qualified instructors.
Squad drill without arms	8	
Squad drill with arms	7	Rifle to be issued.
Musketry	14	
Marching order ...	2	
Lectures	3	
Total	44	

Employment.	Hours.	Remarks.
Third Fortnight.		
Physical training ...	10	Physical training under qualified instructors.
Squad drill	13	
Musketry	13½	
Extended order drill ...	3	
Marching order ...	1	
Night work	1½	*See* Sec. 113. Preliminary recruit training in night work should be divided into short periods of about half an hour each.
Lectures	3	
Total	45	
Fourth Fortnight.		
Physical training ...		Physical training under qualified instructors.
	10	Running training under squad instructors in accordance with the principles explained in "Manual of Physical Training," Section IX.
Running training ...		
Squad drill	10	
Musketry	16	
Extended order drill ...	5	
Marching order ...	1	
Night work	2	
Lectures	3	
Total	47	

Employment.	Hours.	Remarks.
Fifth Fortnight.		
Physical training ...	} 10	As for fourth fortnight.
Running training ...		
Drill	13	
Musketry	17	
Marching order ...	1	
Night work	2	
Guards and sentries ...	2	
Lectures	3	
Total	48	
Sixth Fortnight.		
Physical training ...	} 10	As for fourth fortnight.
Running training ...		
Drill	13	
Musketry	18	
Marching order ...	1	
Night work	3	
Guards and sentries ...	2	
Lectures	3	
Total	50	

Employment.	Hours.	Remarks.
Seventh Fortnight.		
Physical training ...	10	Physical training under qualified instructors.
Squad, platoon and company drill ...	8	
Musketry	10	
Field work, including instruction in night operations	12	
Guards and sentries ...	2	
Route marching ...	5	Marching order, without packs. (*See* Sec. 112.)
Entrenching	2	Recruits should first be taught to construct cover for themselves with the entrenching implement and then to improve it gradually with the entrenching tools.
Lectures	3	
Total	52	
Eighth Fortnight.		
Physical training ...	10	Physical training under qualified instructors.
Squad, platoon and company drill ...	8	
Musketry	10	
Field work, including instruction in night operations	12	
Guards and sentries ...	2	
Route marching ...	5	Marching orders.
Entrenching	3	
Lectures	3	
Total	53	

Employment.	Hours.	Remarks
Ninth Fortnight.		
Physical training ...	10	Physical training under qualified instructors.
Drill	8	
Musketry	10	
Field work, including night practice and outposts	10	
Route marching ...	6	Marching order.
Guards and sentries ...	2	
Bayonet fighting ...	5	
Lectures	3	
Total	54	
Tenth Fortnight.		
Physical training ...	10	Physical training under qualified instructors.
Drill (including ceremonial)	8	
Musketry	10	
Field work	10	
Route marching ...	6	Marching order.
Entrenching and elementary field works	3	
Bayonet fighting ...	5	
Lectures	3	
Total	55	

Eleventh and Twelfth Fortnights as for Tenth Fortnight.

2. *Lectures to recruits.*

1. Lectures should frequently be delivered by officers ; with a view to retaining the attention of the recruits they should not as a rule exceed half an hour in length, should take place at suitable hours, and should be made as attractive as possible.

2. The lectures at the commencement of the recruits' course of training should be mainly on elementary interior economy, sanitation, discipline, regimental distinctions, the meaning and importance of a military spirit ; subsequently they may also be on the work of the period, and should then if possible be illustrated by incidents taken from actual warfare, which should emphasise the value of a military spirit in war.

Some time during the lecture hour should be devoted to catechism on previous work and lectures.

3. The following are some of the subjects suggested as suitable for lectures to infantry recruits :—

Barrack room duties.   Cleanliness and smartness expected from the soldier.   Dress and clothing.   Local orders.   Good name of the regiment and army.   Conduct when out of camp or barracks.   Position of provost, and duty to obey and support him.   Duty when ordered as escort.   Names, rank, and position of officers.   Regimental colours.   Saluting.   Manner of making a complaint.   Reporting sick and hospital rules.

General conduct while in the army.   Immediate physical and material advantages of moderation and sobriety.   The advantages of physical fitness.   Prospects of civil employment in after life affected by conduct while in the army. Registration for employment dependent on good character on discharge, preference being given to exemplary or very good characters.   For police or post office employment an additional certificate of absolute sobriety is necessary.

Fitting equipment. Laying down kits. Marching order. Hints on marching ; boots, socks, clean feet, treatment of blisters. Drinking on the march.

Falling out. Instances of long marching and endurance. Sanitation and hygiene.

The rifle and elementary theoretical instruction in musketry.

Duties on guard.

Movements in extended order and use of the rifle.

Co-operation, comradeship, disregard of self and their importance in war.

Observation and the use of the ears and eyes by day and night.

(NOTE.—No reference to drill movements is made in
this index. Headings of sections dealing with
drill will be found in the contents.)

INDEX.

A.

D.

G.

H.

O.

S.

T.

W.

www.ingramcontent.com/pod-product-compliance
Lightning Source LLC
Chambersburg PA
CBHW030408100426
42812CB00028B/2878/J